How can I live with my unsaved husband?
Who provides headship for the single woman?
What does it mean to be sexually fulfilled?

These are just a few of the questions Rita Bennett tackles in the revised and updated *I'm Glad You Asked That.* If you're wondering how God wants you to face the specific situations in your life every day, then you've come to the right source. Here Rita Bennett shares fresh insights, revealed to her by the Holy Spirit, that delve into the heart of the issues that women have on their minds. Her style is delightfully direct and loving. Her answers, written from a godly viewpoint, cover major passages in the Bible concerning women. You'll learn how to be confident that the steps you take to handle daily situations are following the path of Jesus Christ.

BY Rita Bennett

Emotionally Free
I'm Glad You Asked That

COAUTHOR With Dennis Bennett

The Holy Spirit and You
Trinity of Man

Rita Bennett

I'm glad you Asked That...

Fleming H. Revell Company
Old Tappan, New Jersey

Library of Congress Cataloging in Publication Data

Bennett, Rita.
     I'm glad you asked that.

     1. Women—Religious life. I. Title.
BV4527.B43   1983   248.4′83043   83-3311
ISBN 0-8007-5111-6

With great love to my husband, Dennis, who keeps me
"glad he asked that question"

CONTENTS

HEADSHIP

GROOMING

PROBLEMS

SPIRITUAL LIFE

Preface

Here is the revised edition of *I'm Glad You Asked That*. It is truly revised. I have gone through it carefully, and made a number of changes, small and large. Some material has been deleted, because it is not relevant today.

When this work was first published in 1974, extreme teachings were being expounded about woman's place in church and home. As I autographed the book at the Christian Booksellers Association convention that year, I felt somewhat of a maverick. In fact, one man smiled at me and told me just that. I felt perhaps he should smuggle my book home in a plain-brown paper bag for safety! The extremes have not entirely disappeared from the scene; there are still those who try to apply biblical principles as though all the social rules of the Old Testament could be literally applied today. Desiring to follow God, but ignoring the lessons He has taught through human history, they end by putting themselves and others into bondage.

There's a healthier viewpoint on woman's role these days in most quarters. In general, things seem to have moderated, and casualties are now on the mend, finding they are real people with real identities.

In the world, of course, there is great demand for women's rights. Some of the claims and aims are fully justified. The cries do indicate there is real pain present. Women are treated unjustly in many ways, and that needs to be corrected. But some are trying to sweep all traditions out the door, saying, "Women can do anything men can do, and we're out to prove it!" "There are no standards or guidelines, your decisions depend on your situation," some say.

Christian women need to look to Jesus for balance and be careful not to follow extremists in either direction. Let the peace and love of God and an intelligent understanding of Scripture give you inner confirmation of the right path.

Most of the questions dealt with in this book have come from speaking to women's groups, and sharing with my husband, Dennis, in radio programs in Los Angeles and Seattle over a period of eight years. Other questions have come from letters and from personal counseling. I've tried to deal with most of the scriptural issues concerning women, as well as the questions women frequently ask about interpersonal relationships.

I enjoyed doing research for the answers, and the fresh, new understanding given directly by the Holy Spirit. This book is written from a Christian standpoint, but I trust others will find it helpful.

I hope that after you've read *I'm Glad You Asked That* you'll say, "I'm glad I read that!"

RITA BENNETT

Acknowledgments

I have dedicated this book to my husband, Dennis, and I want to thank him, too, for his painstaking help in the revision of this book. We have coauthored books, and written books individually, but we always work together, generally supporting one another in the demanding and exciting work of writing.

To Pat King, and Jo Anne Sekowsky, love and thanks in the Lord for their help and encouragement during the writing of the first edition of this book. Loving thanks to our friend and former secretary, Janet Koether, who typed the first edition of this book, and also this revised edition. Thanks, too, to Sue Williams, our friend and secretary, for her support and conscientious help.

Loving appreciation to all the friends who pray for us and for our ministry of writing.

Much appreciation to the editorial staff at Fleming H. Revell Company, for their confidence in this book, and for their always pleasant and patient help and counsel.

Above all, praise and glory to Jesus, the One who is the Answer to all our questions.

THE SINGLE GIRL

1

Isn't Virginity Old-Fashioned?

Dear Rita,

What's the good of being a virgin before marriage? It seems that only puritanical people think such a standard is important anymore. Recently a minister told a friend of mine that marriage will be outmoded in the next ten years, so it won't matter anyway. So many books, movies, and magazines encourage free swinging love today, that I'm beginning to think I've been rather square. Do you think Christians should change with the times?

Dear Rather Square,

When Paul teaches about marriage, he compares it to the relationship between Jesus and His people. In Scripture, God uses the picture of marital fidelity as a type of His faithfulness, and/or His people's faithfulness or unfaithfulness to Him. In the Old Testament, polygamy is tolerated—a man may have more than one wife—but this is far from God's original plan of one woman for one man. There is, however, *no toleration of premarital sex in the Bible.* You will not find in Scripture any example of the kind of relationship that is often taken for granted today, in which a couple who are not even necessarily intending to marry have sexual intercourse simply as a part of the dating process; or that couples should live together and have sexual relations, but not get married.

Incidents of sex outside marriage in the Bible involve either prostitution, rape, or adultery. It is never a normal and accepted part of life. Amnon, one of King David's sons, thought he was in love with Tamar, his half-brother Absalom's sister (2 Samuel 13). He tricked her into taking care of him during a feigned illness, and then forced her to have sexual relations with him. He immediately turned against her, hating her more than he once thought he loved her. Amnon's so-called love was only selfish sexual desire. He was willing to harm her emotionally for a moment of temporary satisfaction. The situation was compounded when David's son Absalom, resenting his father's failure to punish Amnon, took revenge by having Amnon murdered, and then went on to rebel against David.

Then there is the savage story of how Shechem the Hivite seduced Dinah, Jacob's daughter. The pagan prince took Dinah, "lay with her, and defiled her" (Genesis 34:2). Shechem wanted to marry her, but the sons of Jacob were so furious when they learned what had happened to Dinah that they killed Shechem and all the men of the city and brought their sister home.

The uncompromising attitude of the Old Testament toward sex outside of marriage wasn't because of a prudish or puritanical attitude toward sex. Sex was considered good and to be enjoyed, but it was sacred, and carefully regulated and controlled, because it was vital to the propagation of the race and the strength of the family.

No Double Standard

The Bible does not encourage a double standard of sexual behavior. Men are to keep themselves for their wives, just as women are to keep themselves for their husbands.

Premarital sex in the modern sense is not rape, since both parties are consenting, nor is it prostitution, since no one receives pay for his or her action. It is not adultery, if neither of the participants is married to someone else. It is often referred to as "fornication," although this word can also be used of adultery, and in the Scripture refers to any kind of sexual misbehavior. (The Greek word for it is *porneia,* from which we get the word *pornography.*)

Some may think the Bible is too narrow, but there are plenty of reasons for prohibitions against premarital sex. Sex is not an end in itself, but is an expression of true love and fidelity. It can rightly be engaged in only within the bonds of the marriage vow. In so-called free love, the woman is always the loser. Modern "freedom" of sex really means the man is free to get the gratification he wants without any responsibilities to go with it. The girl wants love, companionship, warmth, and out of this will grow the ability to respond, and have sexual satisfaction within the safety of marriage.

Modern contraceptives have led many to the conclusion that it is all right to have sex without marriage, since the fear of getting pregnant has been removed. But a girl who is persuaded to have sex on a date is usually cheated in more ways than one. She will rarely enjoy the experience as she should, because a woman needs to feel secure in order to respond properly, and the date situation will probably be fraught with anxiety. The man has his kicks, because sex is a more external thing to him—he does not have the same inhibitions. However, both persons are harming themselves psychologically and spiritually.

Don't let anyone talk you into it. If a man doesn't want you for yourself, if he doesn't love and care enough to wait for marriage, don't be persuaded to give him your body for his use. I agree with Shirley Boone, who says in her book *One Woman's Liberation,* "The only free love around that I know about is described in John 3:16: 'For God so loved the world that He gave his only begotten Son, that whosoever believes in Him should not perish, but have everlasting life!' "

But What If I Already Did?

What of the people who have already gone this route, who have already been taken in by the "new morality" (which is simply the "*old* immorality") and have been promiscuous with a number of partners. Are they ruined?

The wonderful thing about Jesus is that when we turn to Him and ask to be forgiven, He cleanses us from all sins, big and little, and makes us into new creatures. He not only forgives our sins but forgets them.

An outstanding picture of the grace of God is shown in the story of the prostitute Rahab in Joshua 2–6:25. When the children of Israel were coming to Jericho to possess the land promised to them, they sent two spies to investigate and see how difficult the job would be. The two spies lodged at Rahab's house, which was situated on the wall of the city. (This does not imply the men were seeking her services as a prostitute. Probably she ran an inn or hotel which was the closest lodging inside the gate of the wall.) The king suspected where they were and sent some soldiers to capture them, but Rahab, who came to believe in their God, hid the spies. As a result, they promised to save her and all her family if she would tie a scarlet rope in her front window, the same rope with which she helped them escape over the wall. (This scarlet rope can be seen as a symbol of the blood of Jesus, whereby all who believe in and receive Him may be saved.) Rahab was not only saved physically in the destruction of Jericho, but her previous life was also forgiven. Later, she married an Israelite named Salmon, became the mother of Boaz, who in turn was the husband of Ruth, and the grandfather of King David. Rahab, the harlot, forgiven, became an ancestress in the direct line of the Lord Jesus Christ Himself (Matthew 1:5). She is recorded in what some have called "God's Old Testament Hall of Fame," the eleventh chapter of Hebrews, as one of the commendable women (Hebrews 11:31). The story of Rahab and what God can do in a repentant life should encourage any who have had a checkered past.

What about the man you plan to marry? Is it all right to have sex with *him* beforehand? If you are invited to a banquet, would you think it all right to insist on eating dinner beforehand? Why not wait for the celebration? Why do something that will take the edge off the joy of your marriage? Then, too, if your fiance loves you, will he demand that you cohabit with him before marriage? The fact that he might suggest it does not prove he does not love you, although it might show him to be thoughtless, or even blindly going along with the thinking of the crowd. Maybe he has been taught the popular but mistaken idea that a man "must have sex" in order to be healthy. If you refuse him and he leaves, you will know that he did not really love you anyway.

I believe we should observe scriptural guidelines rather than the thinking of a fallen world. Many young people are floundering for lack of standards. You are told to "do your own thing," but you will have much happier memories, fewer psychological scars to be healed, and will derive deeper enjoyment from your marriage if you will keep yourself for your own husband.

No, Christians should not change with the times, but rather should change the times to fit into God's plans and purposes.

2

Where Can I Learn About Sex?

Dear Rita,

I'm a Christian, twenty-one years old and engaged to be married. I have had very little sex education and don't feel prepared for the physical part of marriage. My mother, minister, and medical doctor haven't given me any practical advice. All my doctor did, in addition to giving me a physical examination, was to suggest birth-control pills if I wasn't interested in having children right away. I know books on sex are all over the bookracks, but I'd be embarrassed to buy one of them, and if I did, I would not be sure whether it had a Christian viewpoint. Can you help me?

Dear Engaged,

Christians have often fallen down in their responsibility to provide sex education for young people. Most Christian books written in this field in the past have been idealistic but not always practical or truly helpful. I'm glad to say, however, there is now an increasing number of concerned people tackling this subject, braving the prudery and puritanism which sometimes has surrounded it, and coming up with some excellent books.

I have been impressed with the book *I Married You*, by Walter Trobisch, published by Harper & Row. Mr. Trobisch, a European pastor and marriage counselor, talks about the problems of courtship and marriage in a refreshing and candid way. His book is based on real life problems which confronted him when he was asked to speak on Christian marriage to a church congregation in Africa. Another book by the same author is called *Please Help Me!* It presents a Christian view of contraception.

Tim and Beverly LaHaye have written a very good book, *The Act of Marriage* (Zondervan), which I recommend especially for those about to be married and newlyweds. The LaHayes have another book which ranges from courtship and marital happiness, to adjusting to children. It has the somewhat ironic title *How to Be Happy Though Married!* (Tyndale House).

I would also recommend *Sexual Happiness in Marriage,* by Dr. Herbert J. Miles (Zondervan); *Intended for Pleasure* (Revell) by Ed Wheat, M.D. and Gaye Wheat is the best book I've seen to explain how both partners can attain sexual satisfaction.

There are many other books, of course; this is just a sampling. If you apply the truths found in these books, you and your husband should have a good beginning for a successful marriage.

3

How Can I Meet the Right Man?

Dear Rita,

I'm a college graduate in my early twenties. Several years ago, I received Jesus as my Savior, and a short time later as Baptizer in the Holy Spirit.

I am a schoolteacher who finds it difficult to meet eligible young men to date. Those who have invited me out are not Christians, much less living in the power of the Holy Spirit. Like many women my age, I long to be happily married, to have a family, and a place of my own. At present I'm dating a young businessman who is agnostic but claims he doesn't mind if I practice my Christianity. Our friendship has been growing over several months.

I'm aware the Scripture warns against being unequally yoked together with unbelievers, but what if "Mr. Right" never comes along, and I'm left in the lurch?

Dear Teach,

The most important thing for you to decide is whether you want God's first plan for your life, or something less. A woman can go on with God while married to an unbeliever, but it's not easy. There's a part of yourself which you can't share with your husband, and although you can be one in soul and body, you cannot be one in spirit.

Not long ago, an older woman shared with me the story of

her early life. She said she had been raised in an isolated small town where eligible men were scarce. She began dating a young man who could talk the Christian lingo but seemingly had no experience of God. Because of the hypocrisy in the lives of some people close to her, and because she was dating this man, she began to cool down in her own dedication to Christ. One night she had a dream or vision of a handsome young man, and was shown by the Lord that this was the one she was meant to marry. As time passed, she increasingly doubted the possibility of this occurring and, in haste, married the hometown man she had been dating. Three weeks later, a handsome young evangelist came to the little town, the grandson of a famous Christian leader. She recognized him as the person God had shown her in the dream—the man *He* had planned for her to marry. The young evangelist told someone that if he had arrived three weeks before, her last name would have been his!

The man she did marry turned out to be an alcoholic who would regularly leave home, and who made her life and the lives of their children miserable much of the time. She was an accomplished musician (as also was the young evangelist of her vision), but instead of her musical talent being used for God through the years, she had had to wait until the senior years of life to share her talents worldwide. What misery could have been averted, what joy could have been received, if she had not been in a hurry to get married! As the saying goes, "There's something worse than not being married—and that's being married to the wrong man."

Look at the Scripture

Perhaps it would be a good idea to look at the Scripture to which you referred in your letter *in toto:* "Be ye not unequally yoked together with unbelievers: for what fellowship has righteousness with unrighteousness? And what communion has light with darkness? And what concord has Christ with Belial? or what part has he that believes with an infidel? And what agreement has the temple of God with idols? For you are the temple of the living God; as God has said, I will dwell in them, and walk in them; and I will be their God, and they shall be my people" (2 Corinthians 6:14–16, author's paraphrase). Although these verses are not referring specifically to marriage, they are certainly applicable to it as well as to other personal relationships.

Another significant Scripture is, "Jesus . . . said . . . Every kingdom divided against itself is brought to desolation; and every city or house divided against itself shall not stand" (Matthew 12:25).

There are enough things to adjust to in marriage without inviting the obvious problems that come from being unequally yoked. Even in a marriage between two believing Christians, there are plenty of adjustments to make. My further advice to you, and other young women who are baptized with the Holy Spirit, is to marry a man with the same experience, and who wants to live in the freedom of the Spirit. For me, there would be something lacking in our marriage if my husband and I could not pray and sing daily in the Spirit together, as well as share in Bible reading, prayer, and praise. The husband should be the spiritual head of the home and take the responsibility for daily family worship. It's a good idea to begin the practice of shared prayer and Bible reading during courtship.

A young woman from our church was seriously dating a young man, and it looked as though their engagement would soon be announced. Fortunately, our young adult group was studying Scripture and discussing what Christian marriage should be like. When this girl saw the verse about wives being expected to submit to their husbands "as unto the Lord" (Ephesians 5:22), she realized to do that she would have to have confidence in her proposed husband's relationship to the Lord. Because she did *not* have that confidence, she ended the relationship. The right man for her came along later that year, and now she is happily married.

Tell Him About Your Faith

Have you told your agnostic suitor about your experience of Jesus? An agnostic, you know, is not an atheist; he simply doesn't believe it is possible to know about God. Your friend may be hungry to find out what you know. Share some good books with him, books of testimony like my husband's *Nine O'Clock in the Morning,* or Pat Boone's *A New Song.* Buy him C. S. Lewis's *Mere Christianity.* Have you invited him to your church and/or prayer group? See if he has any openness to the Lord, and give him the opportunity to receive the same new life and power that you have. If he shows no interest, you would be wise to lovingly but firmly end your relationship with him.

How are you going to meet men who have the same faith as you? Get involved with a home prayer group open to the gifts of God's Spirit and under responsible leadership, or help to get one started for people your age. Some churches sponsor groups for young unmarried people which you can attend without being a member of that church. Often these are held in restaurants or on other so-called neutral ground. The denomination your husband-to-be comes from is not as important as that *he has accepted Jesus,* and is empowered with the Holy Spirit.

Jesus said, "Seek ye first the kingdom of God . . . and all these things shall be added unto you" (Matthew 6:33). If you put God first in your life, the other things will be added. If you put marriage first, you may miss God's best plan for you. God wants you to be fulfilled—spiritually, mentally, and physically!

God has given you a desire to be married, and I believe He will fulfill that desire if you are patient. Don't let the enemy scare you with the idea that you'll lose out if you don't accept the first available male! Remember, the enemy drives the sheep, but the Lord Jesus leads them.

Trust the Lord, and also use the common sense He has given you! Keep your weight normal, and dress and groom yourself attractively. And there's nothing wrong with taking the opportunity to be in places where there are eligible males. I believe I'm not wrong when I say, "Mr. Right will be along, and at the right time too!"

4

How Can I Receive the Power to Say *No?*

Dear Rita,

I am a junior in college and have been secretly in love with, and sneaking off to date, one of my professors, a married man. We haven't gotten to the point of having an affair, but we're headed in that direction. I've heard that the Baptism in the Holy Spirit can make God's power more real in a person's life, and I wonder if this might be what I need to be a stronger Christian, and resist things that I know are wrong. I want to pray for this experience with God, but know I can't while living out of His will for my life. What can I do? I really love this man, but I also love Jesus, and I know He wouldn't want me to keep on in this relationship.

Dear Tempted Co-ed,

The very fact that you've asked this question shows that the Holy Spirit is at work. I'm sure you've already realized that you'd never be truly happy sneaking around as mistress to your professor. I'm also sure you wouldn't want to cause the breakup of his marriage.

Often young women who have not received normal love and affection in formative years are easy prey to men who are more than willing to meet their need for love. I don't know if this fits you or not, but if so, Jesus is the only One who can truly meet the deep need you have to be loved. To paraphrase Saint Augustine, "God has made you for Himself and you'll be restless until you find your rest in Him." And receiving the Baptism with the Holy Spirit is the best way I know for you to strengthen your experience of God. It will make you more aware of God, and heighten your fellowship with Him. It will fulfill your life in a new way. This is why some people call it a baptism of love. (Let me explain here that I use the terms "Baptism *with* the Holy Spirit" and "Baptism *in* the Holy Spirit" interchangeably, since *in* and *with* are interchangeable in the Greek.)

Jesus knew people would have great temptations, and He did not leave us powerless against them. After His Resurrection He breathed the Holy Spirit into His first followers (John 20:22), but He still commanded them to wait until they had received the *Baptism* with the Holy Spirit before they went out to tell other people about Him (Acts 1:4, 5). They were already born again of the Spirit, but they hadn't received the *power* Jesus knew they would need. Jesus' final recorded words on earth were, "But you shall receive power when the Holy Spirit has come upon you; and you shall be My witnesses both in Jerusalem, and in all Judea and Samaria, and even to the remotest part of the earth" (Acts 1:8 NASB).

Jesus' Last Orders

You'll understand how important the promised empowering of the Holy Spirit is if you think about these final instructions Jesus shared with His first disciples. He knew they were going to need *power* (Greek, *dunamis,* from which we get our word *dynamite*), in order to make it as witnesses. If you were chosen to travel to the moon, your final words to your friends and family just before you blasted off would be well chosen, wouldn't they? They wouldn't be about trivia, but helpful and important. That's the way it was with Jesus.

Luke tells about it at the beginning of Acts. He says it in a slightly different way in his version of the Gospel, "And behold, I am sending forth the promise of My Father upon you; but you are to stay in the city until you are clothed with power from on high" (Luke 24:49 NASB).

Many young people in circumstances like yours would have been saved tragic mistakes and heartaches if only someone had told them about the power of the Spirit. It is sad to see young people led to know Jesus as Savior but not told how to ask Him for the power to live the life. It's much like sending a soldier into battle, but not giving him weapons.

I'm glad someone told you about the Holy Spirit's power, so the tragedy you were headed for will not occur. You've already made your choice for Jesus by your request for advice. Rather than trying to tell you in this letter how to receive the Baptism with the Holy Spirit, I recommend that you read the first five chapters of our book *The Holy Spirit and You,* which tells all about it in careful detail (Dennis and Rita Bennett, published by Bridge Publications). If you can find someone to help you pray, that's fine, but you can pray by yourself, since you've accepted Jesus, and He is the One who baptizes in the Holy Spirit.

After receiving the power of the Holy Spirit, your most active defense against the enemy and his temptations will be to stay in close fellowship with God and empowered Christians. Attend a Spirit-filled prayer meeting at least once a week. Read the Bible, to get guidance for your life. If you don't have one, buy one of the modern translations, and use it along with the King James Version. Get into a good Bible-study group, if at all possible, and attend church each week. Receive Holy Communion (the Lord's Supper, the Eucharist) regularly.

Some Dos and Don'ts

Don't talk to your professor in any secluded place. You may want to write to him and tell him what has happened to you. You may want to send him a book about this, such as my husband, Dennis's, *Nine O'Clock in the Morning*. You may be the means of saving this man—and his marriage. A word of warning: if he shows interest in your faith, you are not the person to talk to him! Find someone else, preferably a man, to do this, otherwise you may be drawn back into intimacy, even though your motives are the best.

Avoid going to places that would tempt you to reminisce about some of the good times you had together. Don't listen to music that makes you think of him and pulls at your heartstrings. It may help you to think about this Scripture:

No temptation has overtaken you but such as is common to man; and God is faithful, who will not allow you to be tempted beyond what you are able, but with the temptation will provide the way of escape also, that you may be able to endure it.

1 Corinthians 10:13 NASB

The Lord has provided your way of escape, so take it. As you do, He will provide the right man for you—one who doesn't belong to someone else. Keep yourself for him. You'll be glad you did.

Get ready to blast off into a new dimension in your spiritual life. You'll find that the pull of earth will be less and less powerful as you go into orbit with the Lord!

THE
MARRIED
WOMAN

5

How Do You Get Him to Talk?

Dear Rita,

I have been married for a little over a year, and know I have much to learn about getting along with my husband. Mealtime is supposed to be relaxed and happy, but often at our house it's just the opposite. If I bring up any problem at all, it's usually the straw that breaks the camel's back—just one too many. How am I going to share necessary concerns with my husband when he gets so upset every time I do?

Dear Needing-to-Communicate,

To answer your question, the best scriptural analogy I can think of is how Jesus handled Peter, when He needed to have a little talk with him. Peter, who usually had good intentions, said he was willing to die with Jesus, yet, at the end, he three times denied even knowing Him.

John 21 tells about the third time Jesus appeared to His disciples after His Resurrection. Peter was back at his old trade of fishing. He must have reasoned, *After all, Jesus didn't bring in the kingdom as we thought He would, and I have to make a living some way.* That night the fishing was totally unproductive, but Jesus, standing on the shore, shouted for them to cast the net on the opposite side of the boat. When they did so, the net filled up with so many fish that they couldn't pull it into the boat, but had to drag it to shore. When they realized the man on the shore was Jesus, Peter threw himself into the water and swam to Him.

Jesus didn't immediately say to Peter, "You're just the one I've wanted to see. I'm displeased with you and the way you denied knowing Me. Sit down and let's have a talk." Instead, Jesus said to Peter and the rest, "Let's have something to eat." He knew they were wet and hungry and tired, and He had enough fish for all of them grilling on a campfire. After Peter was well fed, and dried and warmed by the fire, Jesus began to have a talk with him.

A Good Pattern for You

This is a good pattern for you and for all wives. When your husband comes home from a hectic day at work, he needs time to make the transition from his job to his home. Greet him at the door with love and encouragement, and have dinner on time. Keep the conversation light and pleasant during the meal. After he's been well fed and has had some time to relax, *then* share your concerns with him. Always preface the problem, especially if he's in some way involved in it, with some appreciative, relationship-strengthening remarks: "Thanks for taking time to pick up those groceries for me"; "You're a wonderful husband; it was so thoughtful of you to telephone me today." Let him know you love him. In this way, he will not feel so threatened when you bring up the problem.

Jesus not only fed the disciples physically, He fed them spiritually as well. You can feed your husband in the same way. During the day, while your husband is at work, you can be receiving spiritual nourishment from the Lord. Spend time feeding on His Word. Listen to Scripture on tape or taped faith-building teaching and testimonies while you iron, sew, or run taxi service to and from school, or when driving to the grocery store. When your husband comes home from work, he will feel refreshed by the presence of Christ in you. You will find yourself sharing words of life, rather than bits of negative gossip.

Who knows? You yourself may be so refreshed by the heightened awareness of Jesus within you, that even the problem you needed to air will have turned into an avenue of blessing for both of you. As Jesus said, ". . . With men this is impossible; but with God all things are possible" (Matthew 19:26).

All things are possible, even happy meals with joyful fellowship around the supper table.

6

Every Woman Can, But Should She?

Dear Rita,

I've been married four years and have a very kind and loving husband. Recently, through reading on the subject of sexual adjustment in marriage, I came to understand that women, too, were supposed to enjoy fulfillment. Giving myself physically to my husband is nice, and I feel it is my wifely duty, but I never expect more than a sense of belonging, and the satisfaction of meeting my husband's needs. Does this idea of the sexual climax for the wife have a Christian basis or only a secular one?

Dear Dutiful Wife,

There is no truth in the idea that Christianity teaches against sexual pleasure in marriage, and especially that a woman should not enjoy it. The notion comes from the Victorian era, and from a kind of false asceticism which is really from the Eastern religions, rather than from the Bible. Marriage was intended to meet the sexual needs of *both* partners.

One particular confirmation in Scripture stands out in my mind, that of Sarah, Abraham's wife. When she was nearly ninety, long past the menopause, and her husband was nearly one hundred years old, an angel came to tell Abraham that Sarah, who had been barren until that time, would have a son. Sarah, who was in their tent home, overheard

37

the conversation, and the Scripture says, "So Sarah laughed to herself, saying, 'After I have grown old, and my husband is old, shall I have pleasure?' " (Genesis 18:12 RSV).

Apparently Sarah had found the marriage union a pleasurable experience. Yet in the New Testament, Sarah is set up as an example for Christian wives to follow: "For after this manner in the old time the holy women also, who trusted in God, adorned themselves [inwardly], being in subjection [voluntary subjection in love] unto their own husbands; Even as Sarah obeyed Abraham, calling him lord [sir]: whose daughters you are, as long as you do well . . ." (1 Peter 3:5, 6, author's paraphrase).

The clearest New Testament teaching on sexual adjustment is in Paul's First Letter to the Corinthians:

> The husband should give to his wife her conjugal [sexual] rights, and likewise the wife to her husband. For the wife does not rule over her own body, but the husband does; likewise the husband does not rule over his own body, but the wife does. Do not refuse one another except perhaps by agreement for a season, that you may devote yourselves to prayer; but then come together again, lest Satan tempt you through lack of self-control.
>
> 1 Corinthians 7:3–5 RSV

Both Have Needs

This passage says that both husband and wife have definite sexual needs to be met in marriage. The Victorian idea that sex was to be enjoyed only by the man (the wife simply putting up with it), is erroneous in the light of the Bible and of scientific fact. Note that this Scripture doesn't say the wife is to meet *her own* sexual needs, nor does it say the husband is supposed to meet *his own* sexual needs, but it does say that they are to meet *one another's* needs mutually.

The Book of Proverbs puts it beautifully:

> Drink waters out of thine own cistern, and running waters out of thine own well.... Let thy fountain be blessed: and rejoice with the wife of thy youth. Let her be as the loving hind and pleasant roe; let her breasts satisfy thee at all times; and be thou ravished always with her love.
>
> Proverbs 5:15, 18, 19

This passage indicates that in sexual union the husband is to rejoice *with* his wife, which indicates that not just one partner is to enjoy it. Procreation is not mentioned here. From this and many other verses, the Bible seems to be saying that children are an added blessing to marriage, but are not the only purpose for sexual relations.

Genesis tells the first love story: After the woman was created and presented to the man, God instructed them, "Therefore shall a man leave his father and his mother [in the public legal action of getting married], and shall cleave unto his wife [an inseparable love, *keeping only unto her*]: and they shall be one flesh" (Genesis 2:24).

Jesus quotes this passage showing He based His thinking about marriage on it, and adds further, "They are no longer two but one..." (Matthew 19:6a; *see also* Mark 10:8 RSV).

One flesh obviously refers to the physical union of the husband and wife in the act of love. To be one flesh indicates the same experience for both; they should have the same joy in sexual union. To be no longer two but physically one is to know what the other needs and how to satisfy him or her. Again, this passage doesn't refer to reproduction but to sex as a profound personal experience, which can be known at its fullest only in the sheltered bonds of matrimony.

The necessary ingredients for marriage mentioned by

God the Father in the Old Testament, and God the Son in the New Testament are *leaving, cleaving,* and *being one flesh.* If any one of these aspects of marriage is lacking, the marriage is not as complete as God intended it to be.

It's a Learning Process

Learning to enter into a mutually satisfying sexual experience requires knowledge, time, patience, and much love. It's a complex process, which doesn't usually happen by instinct alone. I would encourage you and your husband to work toward the goal of mutual physical satisfaction, because when you really desire and need your husband in this way, he is bound to enjoy the marriage union more also. You and your husband would do well to do some reading together on this subject. (*See* suggested books in chapter 2.)

Of course, a marriage can be fulfilled sexually and still lack fulfillment in the areas of the soul (mind, emotions, and will) and spirit (that part created for fellowship with God). The spiritual joining of a man and wife occurs when they both accept Jesus as their Savior. They are then "joined to the Lord" and become one, not only with Jesus, but with one another in spirit. The Baptism in the Holy Spirit joins husband and wife in an even fuller way in their minds and emotions. Physical union for a Christian couple should therefore be more beautiful and fulfilling than that of a marriage outside Christ.

After all, marriage was God's idea (Genesis 2:18; 1:27, 28) and He saw that ". . . it was very good" (Genesis 1:31). Only He can make it really good in its every aspect.

7

What Else Can I Do to Convince
My Husband?

Dear Rita,

I received a new release in the Spirit six months ago, and I tried everything I could think of to interest my husband in what had happened. I left books and pamphlets on the coffee table and in the bathroom and bedroom. I asked friends to drop in and casually invite us to meetings. I even laid hands on him and prayed for him in the middle of the night! I tried to witness indirectly to him in my telephone conversations with others (hoping he was listening). Now he doesn't even want me to mention the subject. My husband is a professed Christian, and I know how much this experience of the Holy Spirit would mean to him—if he would only open up. He finally went to one prayer meeting, but got so nervous that he had to have a drink afterwards! I'm anxious to know what I can do.

Dear Anxious,

You may have done too much already, but the Lord will help redeem the situation. No blame can be attached to you for trying everything you could think of to interest your husband in the freedom of the Holy Spirit. However, there is a way of the Spirit which will gently guide your husband, or there is the way of man which will push him too fast, and end up causing him to resist and perhaps reject the whole idea.

When I read your question, it reminded me of this story: A man sitting in his garden saw a butterfly emerging from its cocoon. After two hours, the butterfly was only halfway out. Fascinated by the ongoing struggle, the man noted a narrow place that was restricting the butterfly. He took his penknife and cut open the narrow place to help the creature. To his sad surprise, the last third of the butterfly's body was still like a worm, with just stubs for the hind legs!

We cannot push another's spiritual growth. Each must come at his own speed. If you try to force someone to grow, you may harm him. Fortunately, the realm of the Spirit is different from the natural. Although the butterfly's damage could not be reversed, your husband's problem, being spiritual, can be corrected. Our mistakes can be turned to good—if we release them to God—sometimes greater good than if they hadn't occurred.

You need to learn to rest in Jesus and follow the leading of His Holy Spirit. Instead of thinking up things to do or say to interest your husband in spiritual matters, establish an inward pattern of praising the Lord for what He is already doing in your husband's heart. Praise opens up the way for God to work, and keeps you from being uptight, enabling God's contagious love and joy to show through you more easily.

Don't discuss your husband's inner conflicts with the entire prayer group, as this may leak back to your husband and he will never want to visit the group again. If you have a close friend who has proven discreet, you may want to share and pray about these matters with her, in strictest confidence.

Rest on this Scripture, "We know that all things work together for good to them that love God, to them who are the called according to his purpose" (Romans 8:28).

8

How Can I Be a Stay-at-Home and Like It?

Dear Rita,

I have four children and am a high-school teacher. I went back to my job this year, after staying at home for a year, and now my husband threatens me with, "If our children grow up to be delinquents, it will be your fault!" He doesn't want me to continue to work, and we often have heated arguments about it. It's true we don't absolutely have to have the money, but we both enjoy spending it.

I worked hard to put my husband through graduate school and have helped supplement his salary for years. It seems only fair that I should have a right to determine whether I should work or not. It troubles me greatly that I spent many years acquiring advanced training (I have a Master's Degree in Counseling, and also in Education), and now my husband just wants me to stay at home and hibernate, not using the skills God allowed me to acquire.

Dear Working Mother,

I think you should ask yourself, "Do I want to keep my husband happy (and perhaps even keep him at all), or do I want my profession instead?" Since you are married, and have brought children into the world, your first responsibility is to your husband and your children. Everything else must work in harmony with this.

I can understand how you feel, after working to help support the family for a number of years, and then all of a sudden being asked to stop. Making a home for a husband and four children is a full-time job, though, and if you're working away from home, someone is going to be neglected, no matter how hard you try. If your husband is not getting the love and companionship he needs, it may damage your relationship, and even cause him to seek someone else who is more than willing to meet these needs. And what he has expressed about the children just might take place if you're not at home to guide them. Don't risk your marriage and the happiness of your children for your profession.

There are circumstances, of course, that make it necessary for the wife to work, but you say that is not your problem. It certainly isn't worth risking your marriage and your children for a little extra money to spend on luxuries.

Homemaking is much more than cooking meals and maintaining the house in some kind of order. It is more than just being there when the kids get home from school, or when your husband gets home from work. The mother is the queen of the household, and there is deep reassurance to the children, and to the husband, too, in knowing that she is at home while they are out on the job, or at school. The home should be, as the marriage service in the old Book of Common Prayer calls it "a haven of blessing and of peace," and it means a great deal to a child when he's feeling insecure, to know that he could go home, or call home, and Mother would be there. The man has the same feelings, for all wives are also a little bit of a mother to their husbands, just as the husband is rightly something of a father to his wife. She provides the "kiss it and make it well" of a mother, while he provides the strength and protection that is a father's part. This doesn't mean that you have to stay in the house all day and wait for phone calls, but it does mean that your activities should center around home.

God Will Use Your Training

Now, about your training, which you feel will be wasted if
you do as your husband wants you to. God won't waste
something like that. If you willingly concur with your husband's wishes, God will find a way to apply your advanced
training. Perhaps you will be put to work helping your
church with its education program, or somewhere else in the
community picture. You might wind up on the school
board! Perhaps you will find your counseling skills being
exercised in helping troubled people, either through the
church or through some other program in the neighborhood. Maybe you can do counseling at your home. There
are plenty of ways to use your skills without being in
full-time professional practice, and you may find yourself
doing things that turn out to be even more significant and
interesting.

I, too, was a teacher, and later a social worker. My husband, however, like yours, wants his wife at home. I have
never been idle, believe me. For example, shortly after our
marriage, my husband asked me to teach an adult Bible
class, bringing my teaching skills into the picture. Then I
began to write, using the previous experience I had had in
journalism. God will not waste your talents—He may develop new ones!

Suggestions for You to Consider

Homemaking can be challenging, fulfilling, and creative.
Every wife could make a hobby of nutrition and cooking,
preparing appetizing meals, designed to keep her family
healthy, not just throwing the quickest edible things on the
table. Children love to be greeted by the fragrance of home-
made bread baking, as they arrive home from school.

Vegetable gardening is another worthwhile hobby that benefits the whole family. Take time to redecorate unattractive areas of your home and to shop for the best bargains. Visit your neighbors and invite them over for coffee and fellowship. Maybe you can start a home Bible-study group, and use your teaching ability there.

If you have a flair for writing or sewing, you can try out these talents while the children are in school. Take a course in a creative craft—decoupage, collage, flower arranging. How about enrolling in a nearby college's foreign-language class?

Don't try to do *all* these things, of course; that might leave your family in worse shape than if you were working at a job away from home. But investigate some of them to see what you might like.

Some husbands don't mind a working wife, but yours does, and pleasing him should be your first consideration. The Scripture says, "Wives, be subject—be submissive and adapt yourselves—to your own husbands as [a service] to the Lord" (Ephesians 5:22, 24 AMPLIFIED).

If your husband is willing, you may be able to return to your profession someday after your children are grown up. You will never regret the years spent at home. Trust God, yield to your husband, and see what exciting adventures are in store for you.

9

Must I Continue Working Because My Husband Insists on It?

Dear Rita,

I am a working wife, but I don't want to be. My husband insists that I continue my job. I have worked away from home all our married life, about twenty-five years now. There are so many other things I would like to be doing, but I'm stuck in this job. I am so tired of it. What can I do?

Dear Stuck-in-the-Job,

There are a lot of wives who would like to get a job but their husbands don't want them to. Your problem is just the opposite.

Perhaps your husband is insecure, and doubts whether he can provide for the family adequately without your help. He may be afraid there will not be enough provision for the years after retirement. Your wish to be at home is normal, but under the circumstances, probably the best thing you can do is accept the fact that you must work, and try to enjoy doing it.

Thank the Lord that you have a job. Thank the Lord that you chose a husband who would allow you to work. Ask God to fulfill whatever plan He has in mind for you on this job. Be positive with your husband; tell him you enjoy working, and are glad he is willing for you to do so. (Have a glass of water ready to revive him if he faints!) When your own attitude is right, all kinds of interesting things will begin to happen. You may find your husband's ideas beginning to change, as he gains more confidence in himself.

The Bible Gives Positive Input

Look at two women in the New Testament who had jobs. One was Lydia, a dealer in purple dyes. Paul had been directed in a vision to come to Macedonia, and on his first Sabbath in Philippi, he and his friends found a group of women meeting for prayer on the riverbank. (I used to think that they had come there to wash their clothes, and that the prayer meeting was "unofficial," but the Greek calls it *proseuche,* which means a regular place set apart for prayer, very like a synagogue, except that it seems to have been attended only by women, and was probably outdoors right on the riverbank. Also women had apparently come there for the express purpose of praying; their praying wasn't just incidental to the laundry proceedings, if any!)

Lydia, who was already a worshiper of God, received Jesus and was baptized with her household. It would seem that her home then became the meeting place for the believers in Philippi (Acts 16:40). This church, which began from a group of women meeting to pray, was, as far as we know, the only one in which Paul found no fault, which is pretty good since his letter to them was written after they had been meeting for ten years! We can imagine what a witness Lydia must have been in her business following her conversion.

Priscilla (or Prisca) was another working wife (Acts 18:1-3). She and her husband, Aquila, worked together for years in the "tent and awning" business. Priscilla and Aquila met Paul in Corinth. They had been forced to leave their home in Italy, because the emperor had issued an edict that all Jews must leave Rome. Hearing of their plight when he arrived in Corinth, Paul went to see them. It was because of their business—Paul being of the same trade—that he stayed with them. From that time, they worked together off and on, and Priscilla and Aquila traveled with Paul, frequently having a church in their home. They were close friends throughout Paul's life, and it was their jobs that brought them together.

Have you read Proverbs 31, which tells in detail what an ideal wife is like? I think it would be an encouragement to you. One particular portion stands out for you: "... she worketh willingly with her hands" (v. 13). Don't forget that the Lord wants all that you do to be *willingly done,* as unto Him.

> She is like the merchants' ships; she brings her food from afar. She rises also while it is still night, and gives meat to her household, and a portion to her maidens. She considers a field, and buys it: with the fruit of her hands she plants a vineyard. She girds her loins with strength, and strengthens her arms. She sees that her merchandise is good: her candle doesn't go out at night. ... She makes fine linen, and sells it; and delivers girdles to the merchant. ... She looks well to the ways of her household, and eats not the bread of idleness.
>
> Proverbs 31:14–18, 24, 27, author's paraphrase

These verses make her sound like quite a businesswoman, don't they? She was certainly what we would term a working wife today, and look at the blessings she received:

> Her children rise up, and call her blessed; her husband also, and he praises her. Many daughters have done virtuously, [the Hebrew says "have gotten rich"] but you excel them all. Favour is deceitful, and beauty

is vain: but a woman that fears the Lord, she shall be praised. Give her of the fruit of her hands; and let her own works praise her in the gates.

verses 28–31, author's paraphrase

Don't consider yourself "stuck in a job" anymore, but accept the fact that God has permitted you to be placed there, and thank Him.

10

What About Wife Swapping?

Dear Rita,

My husband isn't "with it" anymore as far as Christianity goes. We are still running with the same friends we used to before we became Christians. These people drink heavily at our parties, and some are now wife swapping. I feel my husband would even like us to get involved in this, if I would consent, but I'm not interested in the wife- and husband-swapping bit. What advice could you give me? I don't have the blessings I once experienced with the Lord Jesus, especially right after I was renewed in the Holy Spirit. Can you tell me why?

Dear Not-Interested,

It's a good thing you're not (interested, that is!), but shouldn't you feel more strongly against this kind of degrading activity? Could it be that the influence from these so-called friends has slowly begun to seep in, so that your new life in Christ is being stifled? The more you expose your mind to the thoughts of unregenerated lost humanity, through constant contact with the friends you speak of—through reading the latest shady novel—or watching television without discrimination—the more your sense of the presence and fellowship of the Lord Jesus is going to diminish, until you may begin to wonder if you ever knew God in the first place.

Satan is a thief and a robber, and he is busily trying to rob you and your husband of the most precious gift of all, fellowship with God. *You can stop this from happening.* Tell your husband if there is wife swapping going on, you want nothing to do with it, or with the people who are doing it. Meanwhile, remember to go the extra mile and submit to your husband in things that are not wrong.

When the Bible speaks of a wife being submitted to her husband, it does not mean he can require her to do something immoral or illegal. She is to be submitted only in that which conforms to God's standards. Ephesians 5 certainly says that a wife should be submitted to her husband "as unto the Lord," but you cannot submit to a husband "as unto the Lord" if he is acting like a pagan and wanting you to do the same. (For further treatment of submission, read chapter 3.)

A Place of Worship

Partner exchanging is wrong. God's pattern from the beginning of creation was one man for one woman. Hear what the Scripture says:

> "Do you not know that your bodies are the members of Christ? shall I then take the members of Christ, and make them the members of an harlot? God forbid. What? Do you not know that the one who joins himself to a harlot [prostitute] is one body? For two, He says, shall be one flesh. . . . Flee fornication . . . he that commits fornication sins against his own body. What? Do you not know that your body is the temple of the Holy Ghost which is in you, which you have of God, and you are not your own? For you are bought with a price:

therefore glorify God in your body, and in your spirit, which are God's.

1 Corinthians 6:15, 16, 18–20, author's paraphrase

There is nothing Satan likes to do more than to defile the temples of the Holy Spirit. A temple is a place of worship, and this is what our bodies are supposed to be—places of constant fellowship with, and worship to God. Even as Jesus Himself had to cast the thieves out of His Father's Temple, so we may have to cast away the works of the enemy from our lives, so that God's presence can once again fill us.

If you find you must go to some of the parties with your husband (without swapping anything), then go wearing the whole armor of God, and have some solid Christians praying for you. Also, remember temperance or self-control is a fruit of the Holy Spirit. Keep your mind clear and unfogged (obviously, stay sober), so God can work through you. Philippians 4:5 says, "Let your moderation be known unto all men. The Lord is at hand."

Get some good charismatic Christian fellowship weekly. *Charismata* is the Greek word meaning, "gifts of God's grace" or "gifts of God's love." The most concise listing of God's supernatural gifts for today is found in 1 Corinthians 12:8–10. They are: the word of wisdom, the word of knowledge, discerning of spirits, gifts of faith, working of miracles, gifts of healing, prophecy, various kinds of tongues, interpretation of tongues. A charismatic Christian then, in the broader sense, is any Christian who believes these gifts are available to the Body of Christ on earth, and is open for any of them to be manifest in his or her life. You need God's gifts to give you power to live in this kind of world.

In a more specific sense, a *charismatic* Christian is one who has experienced Pentecost, as in Acts 2, and is released to express the gifts of the Holy Spirit freely. There is an outflowing of the Holy Spirit from where He dwells in the innermost being of every believer, to baptize or inundate soul and body, and it results in a greater awareness of the Lord and His work.

Pray with the Spirit and with your understanding also, and read the Scriptures each day. Get some good tape recordings and listen to them while you iron clothes or work around the kitchen or drive to the grocery store.

If you do these things, you will not only once again know the presence of God, but your life itself will begin to have an influence on your husband, and even on the people at the parties you attend. They will feel the presence of Christ in you. If these friends don't change, ask God to give you and your husband some new ones. I believe some of your present friends will be asking you to tell them what has made the difference in your life.

11

Is It Unmasculine for My Husband to Cook? (He's an Amateur Chef!)

Dear Rita,

Do you think it is unmasculine for a man to cook or help in the kitchen? My husband likes to cook a meal once in a while as a surprise for me, but a friend says I'm wrong, scripturally, to let him do a woman's work.

Dear Fortunate Wife,

How nice to have a husband like that! Although the kitchen is primarily the domain of the wife, I see nothing wrong with the husband choosing to cook or help with the dishes. I feel sorry for men who have never learned to do anything but boil water. They are helpless when left by themselves and have to rely on restaurant food. It's just good common sense for everyone to know some of the basics of cooking, and after all, many of the great cooks of the world are men.

After escaping from Jezebel, Elijah was sleeping in the wilderness. He was awakened by an angel who provided him with a freshly baked cake and a jar of water and told him to eat. From the context, it sounds as if the angel had just prepared the "cake baken on the coals" which Elijah saw (1 Kings 19:6). In the Bible, angels were not feminine, as in popular religious art, but strong, masculine beings. The cake was so nutritious that after Elijah had slept and eaten again, he was able to journey forty days and nights with no other food. (*That* angel food cake must have been very nutritious! Wish I had the recipe.)

Jesus and His Disciples Liked to Cook

Just before His death, Jesus shared a meal with His disciples. We call it the Last Supper, and it was the traditional Passover Feast, made up of unleavened bread, lamb roast, a salad mixture of crushed apples, nuts and raisins, bitter herbs, greens or parsley, hard-boiled eggs, whole red apples, and wine, according to Ruth Specter in *The Bud and Flower of Judaism.* The place where they met would have had to be well cleaned from top to bottom to make sure there was no speck of leaven, which symbolized sin. Jesus directed Peter and John to make preparation for the feast, and it certainly sounds as though they did the cooking and cleaning themselves (Luke 22:8, 12, 13).

Jesus was the best example of masculinity who ever lived, yet, as someone said, He loved to give bread-and-fish dinners! Twice He fed thousands of people, and then after His Resurrection, he prepared a meal of grilled fish and fresh bread to feed the disciples following their fishing trip (John 21). His manliness wasn't threatened by this. Isn't it possible that Mary, His mother, might have given Him some cooking lessons while He was growing up?

Role Exchanging Harmful

Seriously, I do not like to see the husband staying at home and doing the housework, cooking, and caring for the children while the wife goes out to work. This exchange of roles could be very confusing to children and might cause psychological harm. This reversal of traditional roles could, in time, be harmful to the marriage itself.

Special Situations

There are, of course, special situations, in which it is necessary for the husband to share in, or maybe do the bulk of household work and caring for children—as when the husband is in school and the wife is working to help him complete his education. This, however, should be adjusted to a more normal pattern as soon as possible. If a husband is sick or handicapped, and the wife has to be the breadwinner, he will, of course, do as much as he can to help with the house. If the wife is ill for a period, the husband will shoulder more than the usual household responsibilities, but these are obviously special cases. If husband and wife both decide to work away from home, then they both usually need to pitch in and help with household duties.

You, I repeat, are fortunate to have such a thoughtful husband. Tell your friend that you are so submitted to your husband that you wouldn't think of ordering him out of his own kitchen! And pray for her, as she perhaps has not been so blessed, and may be just a little bit envious!

12

What Will Happen to Our Marriage When the Children Leave?

Dear Rita,

My husband and I have had twenty-two years of happy married life. Now our youngest child has entered college, and we have no children at home. I've been thinking lately about old age and what it might do to our marriage. No relationship can remain stationary, and I am concerned about the future, and what life together will be like.

Dear Concerned,

The story of the marriage in Cana has long been a favorite of mine. You no doubt know it. When the party ran out of wine, Jesus came to the rescue by turning six jars of water into wine. Normally, the last wine to be served was of the poorest quality, but the wine Jesus created at the end of the feast was the best of all (John 2:1–11).

My husband and I were invited to the wedding of two young friends. The minister's talk to them was taken from this story. He said, in effect, "Some people regard the first years of marriage as the special ones, and expect things to degenerate as time goes on. But as the Scripture says, the best wine at the marriage feast was saved for last, so also I believe that in a Christ-centered marriage, God also saves the best for last!" And, may I add, wine does grow better with age.

The miracle at the wedding in Cana, the beginning of Jesus' ministry on earth, was an important occasion. I think the Scripture story is an analogy of Jesus' spiritual union with the Bride of Christ, the Church, assuring that our love and fellowship with Him will grow better and better. Since all marriage should be patterned after Jesus' marriage to His Bride, you should confidently expect that yours, too, will keep getting better.

"The Best Is Yet to Be!"

When you first received Jesus, it was wonderful, wasn't it? Is it any less wonderful now? Will it get even better? Of course it will. Your marriage, then, is a picture of something far greater which is yet to come. As Robert Browning said in his poem "Rabbi Ben Ezra":

Grow old along with me!
The best is yet to be,
The last of life, for which the first was made.
Our times are in his hand
Who saith, "A whole I planned;
Youth shows but half. Trust God; see all, nor be afraid!"

You've had twenty-two years to adjust to one person, and I imagine there were many rough edges worn off both of your lives. You've had many joys and sorrows together. There are beautiful memories, but it's only the beginning. "The best is yet to be!"

13

Should I Force Him to Tithe?

Dear Rita,

My husband is a throw-a-dollar-in-the-plate, nominal kind of Christian. Right now, there is a conflict in our home because I believe in and have been tithing. I maintain that the money is the Lord's, while my husband says it's *his* money. He says by tithing our income, I am hampering his efforts to save for retirement. I'm in a quandary to know what to do! [Note to reader: *tithing* means giving 10 percent off the top of your income to your church. *Offerings* to your church—or other—are over and above this amount. The tithe was an Old Testament rule, but even today we should realize that 100 percent of all we have belongs to God; however, the tithe is still a good basic minimum standard of giving.]

Dear In-a-Quandary,

The Scripture certainly supports you in your desire to tithe. I can understand why it may annoy you when your husband asserts that it's *his* money. *After all,* you may think, *I work hard at home to make it possible for him to go out and earn that money.* And you're right, of course.

However, when you come right down to it, as you say, the money doesn't belong to either of you, but to the Lord. The eternal viewpoint is better. When you tithe, you are giving back to the Lord that which is already His. We brought nothing into this world, and we'll take nothing out of it, except those riches we let God store in our heavenly bank account (1 Corinthians 3:12–15; Matthew 6:19–21). The Scripture says, ". . . for all things come of thee, and of thine own have we given thee" (1 Chronicles 29:14). Since this is true, there is nothing we can actually give the Lord but our love, and this is what He wants most of all.

I can see why you're in a quandary. In fact, you are in the middle of a paradox. The Scripture teaches tithing, and it also teaches the wife to submit to her husband. In your situation you can't do both, but must choose one or the other. Let me ask you, which is most important—to be right (which you are) and force your husband to tithe, or to submit to his decision, have a peaceful home, and by your loving attitude lead your husband to a vital and living relationship with Jesus?

Jesus scolded the scribes and Pharisees because after having been so correct in tithing, even to meticulously giving 10 percent of their spices—"mint and anise and cummin"—they omitted the most important things in the law: love, mercy, faith, and judgment (Matthew 23:23; Luke 11:42). (The Jew saw the word *judgment,* not in a condemnatory sense—a kind of sitting in judgment—but in the positive sense of doing things properly, or knowing the right thing to do in every situation.)

Accept Your Husband's Decision

I believe you should accept your husband's decision in this matter. And be careful not to do so with a judgmental attitude, but with love. After all, God wants your husband's soul, not his money.

Many people, and especially many men, believe that the "church is always asking for money." Your husband may be asking a reasonable question, "Where does the money go when given to the church? How does it help people?" If he is not involved with the church, he may feel his money would be better spent somewhere else.

When your husband truly gives his heart to God, he will *want* to tithe. Then, too, the new wine of Pentecost has a way of liberating the pocketbook!

In the meantime, be sure you are taking an interest in planning for your husband's retirement. Let him know of your genuine concern. Read some good books on this subject. One is *The Most Important Thing a Man Needs to Know About the Rest of His Life* by Ted W. Engstrom (Revell) and another is *Aging as a Spiritual Journey* by Eugene C. Bianchi (Crossroads).

Retirement is a difficult transition for many men, when they may begin to feel very insecure. This is when your role as a helpmate could be most needed. It may be a time when he sits down and evaluates his life and decides he needs to walk more closely with God. Retirement can be the best time of your life together.

A Unique Kind of Tithing

While you're waiting for your husband to allow God to move in his life—and pocketbook—perhaps you can do some part-time work and tithe from what you make by it, if your husband is agreeable. I would not recommend surreptitiously tithing from your grocery or household money, as this would not be an honest way of dealing and would cause more problems when your husband found out.

Your tithing doesn't have to be in dollars and cents. Tithe some of your time in praying for your pastor, his family, and church members in need, or in helping in the church office, book or tape library. Teach Sunday school; sing in the choir; *tithe your talents.* Be expecting God to show you some creative ways to give to your church. He is your real Source of supply, and that supply is unlimited.

Happy tithing!

HEADSHIP

14

How Can My Husband Regain His Lost Authority?

Dear Rita,

My husband is inclined to be passive, whereas I am strong and definite. Because of this, I have tended to be the leader in our family. Recently God has shown me my mistake of domineering in our home, and I'm trying hard to correct it. It's not easy, because my husband has found the passive role requires little effort. As a result of my former attitude, the children don't respect their father, and it isn't going to be easy for him to regain his lost authority. I'm thankful I realized what was taking place in our home before it was too late.

What will happen to our society if men become more and more passive and continue to give up their roles as leaders and heads of the family?

Dear Not-Too-Late,

The third chapter of the Book of Isaiah is highly relevant today. It says, "I will give children to be their princes, and babes shall rule over them . . . the child shall behave himself proudly against the ancient. . . . As for my people, children are their oppressors, and women rule over them. O my people, they which lead you cause you to err, and destroy the way of your paths" (Isaiah 3:4, 5, 12, author's paraphrase).

This certainly pictures what is happening in our society.

We are reaping the results of extreme permissiveness. So many young people have never experienced discipline. Respect for parents and adults in general is often sadly lacking. Some children are allowed to order their parents around, and family life is often miserable.

There are good goals that the feminists are working to achieve, such as equal property rights and credit ratings, equal job opportunity and equal pay, full recognition for the work women do as "ghost writers" and researchers (without the credit going only to men they work for), and so forth. The women's-liberation people are wrong, though, if they teach that a woman cannot find real fulfillment in being a homemaker. I've even heard it said infants and small children should be put into nurseries, so mothers can get out and compete with the men; but this is really fighting against the deepest principles of human nature. The idea that there are no roles in life that are exclusively for men or women is helping to break down the fabric of our society.

Some Men Are Selling Out

As women move into the roles of the men, the men withdraw more and more. As the men withdraw from leadership in the family unit, the wives and children lose respect and love for them. Husbands who don't know God's plan and/or are just too tired and passive to resist, are selling out.

When men fail to take their places as leaders under God, the family unit decays, divorce increases, and marriage itself begins to disappear. The family is the first line of resistance against tyranny; that is why the family is the first target of the dictator, whether from the right or the left. Someone has said, "If men will not be ruled by God, they will be ruled by tyrants." There is a choice to be made.

How can we prevent these things taking over our lives? More women should do as you have done, step back to make room for their men to move forward into their proper roles. Let's help our men to be men.

I'm so glad that you're *not* too late. I trust you'll help open the eyes of other women to what they can do to curb the evil. The Scripture says, ". . . When the enemy shall come in like a flood, the Spirit of the Lord shall lift up a standard against him" (Isaiah 59:19). Let's cooperate with the Holy Spirit to lift the standard high.

15

Who's to Blame That Women Are Still Being Put Down?

Dear Rita:

What is the reason for the big put-down of women? Why is it that women have been in subservient positions throughout history? Who's to blame?

Through the news of TV and radio, and in reading the newspaper and magazines on the subject of women's rights, I've learned that in Africa, even today, the bride is paid for as a common chattel. Orthodox Jewish men still say this morning prayer: "Blessed are Thou, O Lord our God, King of the Universe, who has not made me a woman." In India, congratulations are not given to parents unless the new arrival is a boy. Even in the United States of America, women still characteristically receive less pay for a given job, and have only had the right to vote since 1920. In Moslem countries, especially, women are still barred from voting in national elections. The *World Book Encyclopedia* says this is true of Bahrain, Kuwait, Oman, Qatar, Saudi Arabia, the United Arab Emirates and Yemen. The list of prejudices against women in Christian denominations is too long to go into. I have experienced discrimination in my own church.

All this is getting my dander up! Since listening to and reading recent reports, I'm getting less and less enamored with my life of being chained to this house and our kids.

Dear Put-Down,

In our society, almost everyone is blaming someone else for his or her problems. The institutional Church blames the world, and the world blames the Church. Young blame the old, and the old blame the young. The ecologists blame industry, and industry blames ecology. Labor blames capital, and capital blames labor. The different nations and races continue to blame one another. Women blame men, and men blame women.

Who really is to blame?

Go back to the beginning and see where all the misery started. The story in Genesis of the first man and woman contains spiritual truths that are foundational for the rest of the Scripture. The serpent asked Eve a leading question, "Hath God said ... ?" and implanted in her mind the first doubt about God's goodness and honesty. The enemy went on to imply that God was holding out on His newly created human beings, and that His plans were not in their best interests. The enemy is a smooth talker, and Eve believed him rather than God. She was the first to fall into the trap, and Adam followed. They stopped trusting God. (For a book of Christian fiction that carries out an imagined temptation of the first woman on another planet, read *Perelandra* by C. S. Lewis, published by Macmillan. Dr. Lewis does a marvelous job of enacting an original temptation scene, and through this, not only shows us what the first temptation could have been like, but reveals to us how the enemy continues to work today.)

As He was sentencing the serpent/ Satan for his part in the Fall of Man, God said, "And I will put enmity Between you and the woman, And between your seed and her Seed; He [Jesus] shall bruise your head [a fatal wound], And you shall bruise His heel [a temporary wound]" (Genesis 3:15 NKJB).

Enmity means "a deep-seated hatred." Satan especially hated the woman. She had exposed his trickery (she told on him), and although her gullibility had delivered the world into his hands, the length of his rule would be limited. Through the woman's Seed (Jesus), Satan's doom and the breaking of his dominion were assured.

The Great Hope

The woman, of course, tried to put all the blame on Satan. She was very angry with him, because, originally, she was to have shared dominion with the man in ruling the earth. "And God said, Let us make man in our image, after our likeness: and let them [the man and woman] have dominion over the fish of the sea, and over the fowl of the air, and over the cattle, and over all the earth, and over every creeping thing that creepeth upon the earth" (Genesis 1:26). Now neither one of them would have dominion, and the woman would be ruled over by the man. (The woman was always, from the very first, created to be a helpmate to her husband, and this role has never been changed. A "help meet," as the King James Version puts it, is one who "walks alongside of," and supports.) The one hope she had was that someday a woman would give birth to a Man-Child who would defeat the enemy, and save her and all others who would trust in Him—Jesus the Messiah.

The hatred Satan has for women has been proved throughout history again and again. Most women sense they have an enemy, even though they may not know who he is. When a soldier is on the battlefield, the greatest danger is not knowing who or where the enemy is. Unless women come alive in Christ Jesus, and receive spiritual understanding, they will think it's just the men who are oppressing them. Satan, of course, works through those who are under his control, but when a woman knows the ultimate source of the malice aimed at her, she can, through Jesus, have victory.

I believe Jesus is in favor of women having equal educational opportunities; equal pay, according to ability; the right to be treated as intelligent human beings; the right to vote; and the right to share teaching, gifts, and talents with the Body of Christ. The way Jesus treated women, as recorded in the Gospels, shows that He never pushed them down, but always lifted them up. Mary, the mother of Jesus, says it this way: "For he hath regarded the low estate of his handmaiden: for, behold, from henceforth all generations shall call me blessed" (Luke 1:48). God the Father has regarded or considered the low estate of women in general throughout the ages, and through His Son has delighted in lifting them back up into the position He originally intended for them. In fact, the position is infinitely better for both men and women now than at the beginning, because then we were only His *creatures* and now we can be His *children.* God always makes something better out of our mistakes, if we will only repent and turn them over to Him.

Women Can Hear From God

It is true that there are extreme teachings going around about woman's role, just as there are about other matters. Some even teach that since the husband is the "lord" of the wife, she cannot hear from God, except through her husband. Jesus wants women liberated from such ideas, so that they will realize that they, too, can be used in miraculous ways to express His love and power. He doesn't want His work through them hindered by the idea that they are "mere women."

Christian women who are walking in the Spirit have been restored to equal dominion over this earth. Through Jesus, they have authority over Satan and his kingdom of darkness. Jesus said, "Truly truly I tell you, the [one] believing in me, the works which I do that one also will do, and greater [than] these he will do" (John 14:12 NGT). (The *he* in second half of verse means both genders.) The Christian woman should expect to have authority in Jesus. She may be used to command sickness and disease to depart, to cast out evil spirits, to set the oppressed free, to raise the dead, and to command the wind and waves to obey her. If she is in danger, she may escape from those who would seek to do her bodily injury; she may command a charging wild animal to be still.

I read an article some time ago which told of a woman who was forced into a car by two men, but as she called upon the name of Jesus for help, she was released at the next stoplight.

Some years ago, when I began to pray with people, I was told to be sure always to have a man pray with anyone who needed deliverance, because "the woman was the weaker vessel" (*see* 1 Peter 3:7). (The *weaker vessel* here obviously doesn't mean "less intelligent." It could be referring to several factors: that the woman was weaker as far as the original temptation was concerned, and also that the woman is not as strong physically. This physical strength was no doubt what concerned my friend, but spiritual strength is what matters in such situations.) But the Lord presented me with a person who needed deliverance immediately—prayer to cast out the evil spirits that were tormenting her—I didn't have time to run and get a man, or anyone else! The woman needed help then and there in her wild state; there was no time to waste. I commanded the spirits to depart in Jesus' Name, they obeyed, and the woman was set free. Jesus will use any channel open to Him.

Many women today are being used to heal the sick in Jesus' Name.

The Shared Dominion

Man became the ruler over his wife by reason of the Fall. With a Christian couple, the husband does not "rule" his wife, but receives her as the helpmate she was intended to be, and together they share dominion over the creation.

Some have tried to make it seem that the only directive in the Scripture is that the woman should "submit" to her husband, but Paul also says that we should "[submit ourselves] one to another in the fear of God" (Ephesians 5:21). This speaks to husbands as well as wives. One definition (from the Greek) defines *submission* as "voluntary yielding in love" (Arnt and Gingrich, *Greek-English Lexicon of the New Testament*).

The idea that men and women are equal is not new, but God's own standard, expressed through Jesus Christ, "There are no more distinctions between Jew and Greek, slave and free, male and female, but all of you are one in Christ Jesus" (Galatians 3:28 JERUSALEM). Jesus didn't come to give His life for men only, but for men and women, girls and boys. All God's children are equally precious in His sight, and can bring their needs to Him in prayer at any time or any place. Each person will appear before God, individually responsible for his or her actions in this life.

I hope and pray that your life as a wife and mother will become more and more meaningful to you. It is your first and most important ministry. The shaping of young lives is an awesome responsibility and also can be extremely rewarding for you.

Ask yourself, are the extreme "liberation" people you have seen in the news really happy and fulfilled? Be careful what you watch and listen to on radio and TV. It's important to keep up with the basic news of the day, but to immerse yourself in it constantly is unhealthy. If a TV or radio program makes you feel put down, shut it off.

Pray daily that God will help you be the most effective and beautiful wife and mother possible, one filled with His power and His authority.

16

Do Women Manipulate by Being Submissive?

Dear Rita,

There's a lot of emphasis on submitted wives today, but listening to some of the gals, I seem to hear them saying that obeying your husband is really a way to get him obligated to you so you can get him to do what you want him to. Be sweet and submissive, and you can twist him around your little finger. Do you think this is an honest motivation for being a good wife? Is it Christian?

Dear Desiring-Honest-Motivation,

I think you've put your finger on something here. A woman should not have an ulterior motive in submitting to her husband, or use submission to get her own way.

Because of their historic subservient roles, many women have become master manipulators. Christian women need to be on guard against old, fallen, habit patterns, which would urge them to get their way by manipulating under the guise of submission. Of such women, in 330 B.C. Aristotle is quoted as having said, "What difference does it make whether women rule or the rulers are ruled by the women?" If a woman practices secret rule, she may cause her husband to fall short of God's best.

The Lord sees what she is doing and her heart's motive. 1 Samuel 16:7 says, "... the Lord seeth not as man seeth;

for man looketh on the outward appearance, but the Lord looketh on the heart." A woman should ask herself, "Do I want my own selfish way, or do I want the Lord's blessing?" The two do not go together.

When Jesus proclaimed what we call the Golden Rule, He didn't say, "If you are good to others, they will be good to you." He said, "Whatever you wish that men would do to you, do so to them . . ." (Matthew 7:12 RSV). After you treat them well, they may then proceed to mistreat you, but even so you are to continue to treat them as you would like to be treated.

In marriage, obeying your husband "in the Lord" is not a method for getting him to treat you well, or to do what you want him to; it is just the way God wants you to function. It may not result in your husband's reformation (if he needs it), or his being especially good to you. It isn't a method at all, but obedience to God's law of love. God doesn't indicate that you'll get your way by being nice; the important thing is that you'll be pleasing *Him*.

17

What Can I Do About My Husband's Jealousy?

Dear Rita,

My husband, John, is so jealous. If he had his way, I'd never even be able to call my own sister. I want to do what's right and respect my husband's wishes; yet I don't want to end up with a life that is so controlled I can't even talk to my own relatives. What should I do about it?

Dear Controlled,

Take time to evaluate the reason for your husband's jealousy. Has he always been this way, or has it developed recently? What reasons can you think of for his actions? Is there anything on your part which helped to cause his insecurity? Does he have reason to feel left out when you are with your family? Do they accept him? Can you get them to behave differently toward him, if need be?

If his jealousy seems to be without cause, your husband may need healing in his soul. His insecurity may come from experiences far back in his life, which Jesus needs to heal. If he is an intelligent man—and I am sure he is—try to lead him to see that his behavior is exaggerated, and he needs help to correct it. I recommend you read my book *Emotionally Free,* and other books on what is often called "inner healing"—the healing of the soul or psychological part of us. That book will give you a list of other books to read, too.

Then try to find a church or group in your part of the world that is doing this kind of prayer-counseling.

It may take a while, of course, to get your husband to participate. You may want to get some prayer help for yourself first. Perhaps you can get him to read the books, and then when he sees you are getting help, he will want it for himself.

In the meantime, use your common sense. Avoid doing the things that annoy your husband when he is at home. Ask your sister to telephone you during the day. Try to develop goodwill between your husband and your relatives. Build him up in their eyes, and don't divulge family secrets. Encourage some of your relatives to call up specifically to speak to your husband from time to time, taking an interest in him, too.

I don't have to tell you, I'm sure, to talk to God about all this. He will direct you and give you the strength and understanding you need.

18

Should I Worship My Husband?

Dear Rita,

I know the husband is supposed to be the head of the house, but on the other side of the picture, there are those who almost seem to teach women to worship their husbands! I'm certainly in favor of a right order in the home, but against treating my husband as though he were a little god.

Dear Non-Husband-Worshiper,

I talked to a woman in California recently who said:

"When I hear people teach that a wife should submit to her husband, I have a different picture from most American women. I remember my father as a little dictator who kept my mother and us children completely under his thumb. My mother seemed to worship my father more than God. As a consequence, when I married I was ready to obey my husband's wishes, but I had other problems. I did not know my own self as a person and was afraid to make necessary decisions.

"Fortunately the man I married was just the opposite of my father; he wanted me to develop my talents and abilities as a person, and not simply be an appendage of himself. He respected my opinions and talked things over with me before making major decisions. Because of his love and consideration, we had a very beautiful marriage, and after my husband died, I had the strength to go on living. I had to look for a job, and found one as a dishwasher for a large hospital. Due to the confidence my husband had helped instill in me, within a few years' time, I rose from dishwasher to supervisor. My job requires constant decision making."

Misunderstood Scriptures

Look at a few of the Scriptures which have been misinterpreted by some who teach a kind of husband worship:

Ephesians 5:33 says, "Let . . . the wife see that she reverence her husband." *Reverence* is a word usually used in worshiping God, and so it may sound as though Paul is telling women to treat their husbands like gods. Actually the word as used here means "respect." Paul is really saying, "The wife is supposed to respect her man."

First Corinthians 11:7 says, "Man . . . is the image and glory of God: but the woman is the glory of the man." This is simply reminding women of their place in creation in the physical sense, for other places in Scripture teach that in our regenerated spirits, both men and women are created in the image of God.

In 1 Peter 3:6 we find, "Even as [Sarah] obeyed Abraham, calling him lord. . . ." Notice the *lord* here is not capitalized. When Sarah of Old Testament days called Abraham "lord," it did not mean he took the place of God in her life, but it meant she was showing her husband honor and respect. *Sir* and *lord* are the same word in both the Greek and Hebrew languages. You can tell only by the context in Scripture if it is referring to deity or to man. (The one exception to this is the KJV Bible and some other translations, which sometimes write the whole word in capital letters: LORD. That always stands for the personal name of God.) Today, we reserve the name *Lord* for deity, so it would be more accurate to say Sarah called her husband "Sir."

Some press the example of Sarah, who obeyed her husband, Abraham, to the extent of saying she was his sister (a half-truth, for she was his half sister!) and permitting herself to be taken into the harem of the Pharaoh. God intervened on her behalf, and therefore, the argument runs, women should obey their husbands, no matter what the request is.

But then there's Abigail, in 1 Samuel 25, who specifically deceived her churlish husband and won favor from David (God's choice as king) through it.

What About Extreme Situations?

What about a woman whose husband periodically flies into sadistic rages, and attacks her sexually in such a manner as to cause physical damage? Should she put up with this? What about the husband who demands that his wife have an abortion, or put their child up for adoption? These are all valid questions in this day and age. Should the Christian wife yield to her husband if he insists she perform perverse sexual acts? Or take part in a criminal plot? What if he wants her to get drunk or take drugs with him? The answer is obvious, and certainly those who teach an extreme position on submission would not actually counsel such acts. They are simply idealizing, not thinking the matter through, but such teachings could lead to real harm.

A wife might try to follow her husband's wishes when he's asking something of her that seems to be unwise or unfair, provided it does not violate the law of God or man. But she cannot and should not obey if he wants her to do something illegal, immoral, or unethical. The Scripture says to submit to your husband "as *unto* the Lord" and not "*as* the Lord." True Christian men don't want to be worshiped; they want only to be respected and loved.

19

What About Singles—and Headship?

Dear Rita,

More and more, lately, I've been hearing about the teaching of "headship." It sounds wonderful for women to be able to depend on their husbands to help with major decisions in their lives. However, my situation is different. I'm divorced and have three little girls. Who provides headship for me? To whom can I turn for help and guidance?

Dear Desiring Headship,

For all women without husbands—whether they are single, widowed, or divorced—your pastor, the leader of your church family, can give you headship for your major decisions. You should, of course, belong to a church family where the minister has proven himself to be a godly person, whose conduct is in keeping with the teachings of Jesus Christ. Speaking to men and women in the Church, Hebrews 13:17 says, "Obey those who rule over you, and be submissive, for they watch out for your souls, as those who must give account. Let them do so with joy and not with grief, for that would be unprofitable for you." Verse 7 of that same chapter says further, "Remember those who rule over you, who have spoken the word of God to you, whose faith follow, considering the outcome of their conduct" (both NKJB). When there are major decisions in your life, and when after prayer you still don't know what to do, make an appointment with your pastor and ask his guidance and help. God will often speak through him in a time of need.

A word of warning! This does not mean you're to look to your pastor as your "spiritual husband." (If he's married, his wife wouldn't like that idea either!) Anyone who has done frequent counseling knows of the possible danger of emotional attachment with someone of the opposite sex. Don't think his headship means you are to camp on your pastor's doorstep, asking him about all the minor problems and details in your life. Your pastor is a busy man, and God has given you common sense to make everyday decisions.

Have Three Confirmations

It is good to have at least three confirmations when making a major decision: one could be from the Scripture; another through an inner knowing of right or wrong in your spirit; and another through your pastor. If you're still not sure what to do, fast and pray about it. God may confirm your decision in other ways: through a Bible teaching or a sermon; a counselor who has helped you in the past; or perhaps gifts of the Spirit at a prayer and praise meeting. He may use the words of a friend in a casual conversation. He may use a dream or even a vision.

Best of all, be in tune with the Lord Jesus, so that you hear from Him yourself in the inner witness of your own spirit. There is a real safeguard in asking for several confirmations before making a decision.

Don't try to force God to guide you by "putting out a fleece." I mean, don't ask for a sign that is unrelated to the problem. For example, if you are trying to decide whether to sell a house, it is logical to say something like, "Lord, give me a sign by letting someone offer me a fair price for the place without my having to ask for it." But it isn't logical to say, "Let the right buyer be driving a green Cadillac with wire wheels"! Or, "I'll sell to the first one who arrives wearing a pin-striped suit," or something like that. "Fleeces," like prophecy, need to be handled with care, or they'll get you into a lot of trouble.

God has not left you out, my friend in Christ, but has provided abundantly for all your needs. You are a vital part of the Body of Christ, and Jesus is the Head of the Body, the Church (Colossians 1:18). The Church is also called the Bride of Christ, and Jesus is the Bridegroom. Isaiah 54 is literally speaking of the coming glories of Jerusalem, but spiritually, it has spoken comfort to numerous women who are without husbands. Claim verse 5 for yourself:

> For thy Maker [Jesus—the Creator] is thine husband; the Lord of hosts is his name; and thy Redeemer the Holy One of Israel; The God of the whole earth shall he be called.

Spiritually speaking, Jesus is your husband. Nothing can surpass being a part of the Bride of Christ and being under *His* headship.

GROOMING

20

Do Christians *Have* to Be Frumps?

Dear Rita,

I have a Christian friend who in the past always dressed stylishly and attractively. I saw her recently, and she looked absolutely dowdy. She was wearing plain, most uninteresting clothes, no jewelry except her wedding band, and looked as if she must not believe in going to a beauty parlor anymore. Is this the way we are to look as Christians? She didn't look happy either. In fact, I'm afraid even to phone her, because of her austere look. What do you think has happened, and what will this do to her example to others?

Dear Afraid-to-Phone,

I moved to Spokane, Washington, in 1964, and found many doors open to me to work for the Lord there. This led me to live by faith for finances, so I could give more time to the lay ministry I felt called to. One night I spoke at the home of a Roman Catholic couple. One of the young women there that evening made sure of her commitment to Jesus, and was released in the Holy Spirit. The husband was a leading hairstylist in the area. He was so impressed by what happened to his wife that in gratitude to the Lord he offered to "do" my hair as often as needed. Thus for nearly two years, until I moved to Seattle in 1966, the Lord Jesus not only provided me with a hairdresser but with one that was top-notch. It seemed obvious God wanted me to look my best.

When Dennis and I were speaking at a retreat in Scarborough, Yorkshire, in 1968, a college student told me, "You impress me with the attractive way you dress. So many Christians I've known have tried to be holy by looking as unattractive as possible. I wasn't so sure I'd like being a Christian if I was supposed to look like them!"

I believe we should hit a happy medium. Looking dowdy may be saying, "I don't care enough about others to make the effort to look nice." On the other hand, spending money extravagantly so that we look like clotheshorses won't make a good impression on others, or be pleasing to God either.

I had an experience similar to yours. At a Christian retreat, I met an attractive woman who was newly baptized in the Spirit and very happy. When I saw her again several years later, I hardly recognized her as the same person. She looked pale, unkempt, and awfully plain. Perhaps she was "heavenly minded," but her looks were not a helpful witness for Christ.

Through the years many earnest Christians thought there was something wrong with women making themselves attractive: long-sleeved dresses, drab in color; long hair done up in a bun; pale faces and blue lips. These were the signs of so-called holiness. Fortunately this has changed a great deal, but there are still groups who think and teach this way, and women try to comply, honestly wanting to please God.

Looking Your Best for the Lord

Then there are the women who become careless of their appearance because they are so involved with God's work that they don't give enough time to grooming. Something like this happened to me without realizing it. I used to eat in a certain family-style restaurant in the Los Angeles area. The owner, a Jewish man, was always friendly, and often complimented me on my choice of clothes, and so forth. I had witnessed to him over the months. I was away for a few years, and then returned for a visit. Some friends and I decided to eat supper in my old favorite restaurant. When I said hello to the owner, he didn't seem to recognize me, so before we left, I excused myself and went back to talk to him.

He said, "Yes, I recognized you, but what in the world has happened to you? You used to be such an attractive girl!" I just stood there, gulped, made some lame comment, and then said good-bye.

I was shocked and rather hurt at his response. I had not been aware of the change in my appearance. Extremely busy in the work the Lord had given me, I had temporarily forgotten about the importance of looking my best. My close friends may have thought I looked fine (although even they no doubt would have had more pleasure from my company if I had looked better) but the world evaluates in a different way. My old acquaintance, the restaurant owner, did me a favor to tell it like it was. It was the Lord reminding me that He wanted me to look nice for Him.

A favorite book of mine which will help you select styles and colors to look your best is called *Color Me Beautiful.* The author, Carole Jackson, uses the four seasons of the year to describe people and their best colors. She will help you coordinate your wardrobe, so that you can look good and save money at the same time. Another excellent book on this subject is *Dress With Style* by Joanne Wallace.

What would concern me even more than lack of good grooming is the apparent loss of joy in your friend's life. The same people who encourage a woman to believe she will be more "holy" if she doesn't groom herself stylishly and attractively, often also teach that God is against any kind of joy or fun.

The enemy somehow is robbing your friend. Don't let him continue to rob her—and you, too—by making you afraid to telephone. You need to let her know you are thinking about her and would love to visit with her. Your prayers and loving contact may open doors of fellowship. The Lord then will give you the words to say to help her, I'm sure.

21

Can You Help Me With My Hair?

Dear Rita,

Do you think it's right for a Christian woman to wear a wig, wiglet, or other kind of hairpiece? I'm an outdoors type, love to swim and play tennis. My husband's work is such that I need to be ready to go out with him to dinner and other social functions at a moment's notice. My hair is rather fine and unmanageable, and a wig would be such a help. What do you think?

Dear Outdoors-Type,

Some women are blessed with strong, thick hair, but others have the limp, thin kind, and some may even have problems with baldness. Some are able to work with their hair and comb it into lovely styles, and others are in bad shape the day after going to a beauty parlor! Then there are women like you, always on the go, and wanting to look your best at all times.

I do not see that there is anything un-Christian about wearing a wig or hairpiece. Less than two centuries ago, it used to be the custom for men as well as women to wear wigs, and English judges in court still wear wigs. John Wesley, certainly a great man of the Spirit, wore a wig when he preached in church. It didn't seem to hamper his spirituality or his message.

When a woman knows her hair looks its best, she is more confident and would be more apt to enjoy meeting new people, both in her own circle, and her husband's associates.

If you choose a wig, it should be as close to your own hair coloring as possible, and styled to look like you. In other words, if you're a brunette, I don't think you ought to buy a blonde wig and a red wig, and then surprise your husband and his friends by looking like a different person every time they see you!

Although the fashion for using wigs and hairpieces comes and goes, some Christian women consistently use such helps. The idea is to look as natural, as much like yourself, as possible.

22

To Cut or Not to Cut?

Dear Rita,

I have been letting my hair grow for nearly four years now, but I'm tired of it and in the mood for a change. My husband enjoys my long hair and doesn't want me to have it cut. I'm in a dilemma and need help in making a decision. To cut or not to cut, that is the question!

Dear In-a-Dilemma,

Perhaps you're bored because you lack ideas and new styles for your hair. Try to find a hairdresser who enjoys working with long hair, or talk to a friend who has long hair and knows how to wear it attractively. If your husband wants your hair long, he should be willing to let you purchase the items necessary to keep it well coiffed.

Since you want to please your husband, I would explore changes other than cutting to see if they make you happier. Having your hair shaped to fit your face can give you a pickup. See if there's anything you can do to bring out your hair's best color or highlights. A woman with a long-shaped face should not wear long hair hanging down over the front of her shoulders. Wearing long hair down is fine, until about thirty-five, when it becomes aging. It should then go on top of the head in an attractive style. (When with your husband, in the privacy of your home, you will know how to wear your hair to best please him.)

Recently a friend of mine bought a beautiful thorough-bred dog. His coat was so thick and shiny that I commented on it. She showed me what the breeder told her to purchase to keep his hair that way: wheat germ oil, vitamins and minerals, cottage cheese to be mixed with his meat each day, and I don't know what else! It's surprising how people will make the effort to feed their animals so well, and yet often forget that if those things are good for pets, how good they would also be for human beings. If you want beautiful hair, then, among other things, watch your diet!

Protein shampoos and conditioners are good. Have fun working with your hair and see just how luxurious you can help it become. Take good care of what the Scripture calls your "glory."

23

Should the Eyes Have It?

Dear Rita,

Do you think it is okay for a Christian woman to wear mascara and other eye makeup? I think the emphasis being put on the eyes these days is very attractive, yet recently a minister said it was following Jezebel's example. I certainly don't want to be like her, but at the same time am not sure about the validity of his teaching either.

Dear Not-Sure,

Long, dark eyelashes are a becoming feature. Some people are endowed with them naturally, and others are not so fortunate. If darkening the lashes enhances the beauty of the eyes God created, I can't see any difference between that and wearing attractive clothes, or having your hair styled.

Lining the eyes or applying mascara should be done with discretion, so that it is not obvious. Vonda Kay Van Dyke, former Miss America and a devout Christian, said in her book *Dear Vonda Kay* that some ladies complimented her, "Because it was refreshing to see a girl in her position who didn't wear eyeliner and all that sort of stuff." She thanked them and said, "I do wear it, and the fact that you didn't realize it, is a nice compliment."

Now back to Jezebel. You're right—she's no one to pattern your life after! Yet her sin was not that she "painted her face" (2 Kings 9:30) but that her life was wicked. (In Hebrew, it literally says she "put her eyes in paint"; therefore, this cannot be taken literally as Scripture against rouge and lipstick, as some have used it.) She was a daughter of the Priest-King of Tyre and Sidon, and a fanatical worshiper of the Tyrian Baal. She refused to accept the God of Israel, after she married Ahab, king of Israel, but influenced her husband to allow her god to have equal rights with the God of Israel. She was high-handed, cruel, and unscrupulous, urging her husband in the same direction. God was especially angry when she connived to have a good man, Naboth, killed by stoning—after a mock trial—so that Ahab could get his property. Naboth had previously refused to sell the land because it was his family's inheritance.

She practiced witchcraft, and worked continuously to convert the people of Israel to her faith. She killed all the prophets of Jehovah she could lay hands on.

The prophet Elijah foretold a horrible death for Jezebel, which was fulfilled when Jehu exercised vengeance on the whole family of Ahab. It is at this time the record says that Jezebel "painted her eyelids and fixed her hair" (2 Kings 9:30 *The Living Bible*) before she looked out of the window to taunt Jehu for her husband's death. (This is scarcely mentioned in KJV.) Jezebel was probably not trying to lure Jehu, but rather was showing her defiant vanity. No doubt she always saw to her appearance before she showed herself publicly.

Jehu called on some of the servants who were standing by Jezebel to throw her from the window. When, a little later, Jehu gave the order for the burial of her body, they could find only her skull, her feet, and the palms of her hands—the dogs had eaten all the rest, as Elijah had prophesied

(2 Kings 9:30–37). Her tragic end was not because she wore eye makeup, as some have taught or intimated, but rather to show the end of those who deal unjustly with God's people, follow after false gods, and engage in other evil practices.

Consider the Customs

Certainly it is true that in the Old Testament painting the eyes is mentioned as a way for a woman to attract men for evil purposes (Jeremiah 4:30; Ezekiel 23:40), but it isn't just eye painting that is mentioned, but also wearing gold ornaments (probably referring to earrings), and wearing a crimson gown. All these were simply ways in which the woman was trying to make herself attractive, whether for good or evil purposes. In Proverbs 31:22 we read of the virtuous woman that "her clothing is silk and purple."

The ancient Egyptian and Assyrian women painted their eyes. They blackened the edge of the eyelids, both above and below the eyes, with a black powder called *kohl*. This practice was not as frequent among the Hebrews, but one of Job's daughers was called *Kerenhappuch,* meaning "horn of eye paint" (Job 42:14), indicating that she had lovely eyes.

The time and the custom of the day is an important consideration. Certainly in our time, using eye makeup does not necessarily mean a woman's heart is set to do evil! Not too many years ago, when a woman wore lipstick, it meant she was "on the loose." This obviously is not the case today. It's interesting that while the use of lipstick has been frowned upon by several denominations, those same churches don't have much to say against eye makeup.

The fashions weren't easy on me when I was in high school. Although I learned many good things in the church of my youth, its stand against wearing makeup of any kind was not helpful. In the ninth grade, all the other girls were wearing lipstick. I wanted to wear it too. Because I looked so pale in contrast to the others, I would put it on when I got to school and wipe it off before I got home!

God Loves Me Anyway

Actually being taught that I must not wear makeup did nothing but condemn me and make me draw away from Jesus. If I couldn't keep the rule of no-lipstick, and the many other rules I was supposed to follow, it seemed to me there was no sense in trying to live a Christian life at all. This began for me a wilderness journey which ended in 1960 when I was set free in God's Spirit.

Now that I realize God loves me whether or not I wear lipstick, eye makeup, and fingernail polish, I am actually quite moderate in my use of them.

During years of praying with numerous women, I have seen many tears mingled with eye makeup! If all of them were put together, what a black stream there would be! Some companies advertise waterproof mascara, but I have yet to see it proven. Anyway, I'm glad that mascara is not God-proof, and that He loves all women, regardless of whether they use eye makeup or not!

The Lord Jesus again and again points out that the exterior is not the most important thing to Him, but rather the motive of the heart within. If a woman makes up her eyes to be seductive, the Lord knows that; and if she does it to look more attractive for her husband and her friends, and to be a more effective witness for the Lord, He knows that, too.

What all of us women will find most becoming is to anoint our eyes as Jesus recommended in Revelation 3:18, "... anoint your eyes with eyesalve, that you may see" (author's paraphrase). In the natural sense, eye salve was a preparation used for healing or strengthening the eye. Spiritually, it speaks of healing and restoring our spiritual vision, which was marred by sin.

No matter what we put on or don't put on our eyelids and eyelashes, may our eyelids be open to the vision and understanding God wants us to have, and may our eyes reflect the beauty of Jesus.

PROBLEMS

24

Can I Still Grow Spiritually, Even Though My Husband Isn't Interested in God?

Dear Rita,

I've been married several years. A year ago I met Jesus. My husband is not a believer, and therefore we have nothing in common in this area. I want to grow in the Spirit, and my husband does nothing but hold me back. He doesn't even want me to go to church on Sundays. I've recently come to the conclusion that if I am going to grow spiritually, it will have to be without him.

Dear Held-Back,

Remember you picked your husband, and there must be many things about him which you thought wonderful. You might want to write those things down to refresh your memory. It isn't necessary for you to have a Christian husband in order to grow spiritually. In fact, some people grow faster in the Lord when they are tried, because they have to rely on Jesus more constantly.

Other women have had similar situations. Look at 1 Peter 3:1–3, 4: "In the same way, wives should be obedient to [subject to] their husbands. Then, if there are some husbands who have not yet obeyed the word [that is, they are unbelievers], they may find themselves won over, without a

100

word spoken, by the way their wives behave, when they see how faithful and conscientious they are" (JERUSALEM). (*The Greek-English Lexicon of the New Testament,* Arnt and Gingrich, defines *subject* as "voluntary yielding in Love." It comes from *hypotese,* meaning "obedience" and is used also in Ephesians 5:21 and 1 Peter 5:5.)

You can grow in the Spirit, even though your husband is not yet obeying God or born of the Spirit. In fact, your growth in the incorruptible life God has given you can so transform your behavior, that your husband may be won to God. You are 100 percent correct to desire spiritual progress, but you need to do it in God's way, and according to His pattern.

The husband of a friend in another city began to be infuriated every time his wife went to church on Sunday. She prayed about it, and felt the Lord told her to stop going to Sunday church, but to go instead to weekly prayer and Bible-study groups during the day, while her husband was at work. Her husband was absolutely floored the first few Sundays she stayed home with him. Because she deferred to his wishes, instead of fighting with him, God was able to deal with her husband. After she had stayed away from church for several months, her husband actually began to encourage her to return! I don't know what has happened since, but one thing is sure, their house is not in turmoil on Sundays as it used to be, and her husband is not being encouraged in a weekly habit of getting steaming mad at God! Obviously, any woman who takes this route must be getting Christian fellowship somewhere during this time. If there are any children, she must see that they get to a good Sunday school and young people's fellowship.

The King James translation of 1 Peter 3:1 says the man will be won by the "conversation" of the wife. This is an old-fashioned use of the word. We think of conversation as informal talk, but the Bible word means *behavior* or *conduct.*

You're not necessarily going to win your husband to God by what you say to him, or to others in his hearing. Don't engage in any kind of "spiritual" talk with others that will make your husband feel left out. God understands what you are doing, and won't be hurt if you don't talk about Him at all times! It's what's going on in your heart that's important. The love of God coming through your human nature, without being labeled, is what is going to win your husband.

Don't be discouraged. Jesus found it difficult to deal with His own family, but they all were there on the Day of Pentecost! (*See* Acts 1:14; 2:1.)

Recently, I saw a motto on a banner prettily decorated with orange and yellow flowers, which very nicely capped what I am trying to say: BLOOM WHERE YOU ARE PLANTED. Hold on, Held-Back! You are about to grow like anything, and before long, I believe your husband will be growing right along with you.

25

Can My Pastor Serve as a Substitute Husband?

Dear Rita,

The pastor of our church is a wonderful man who gives unselfishly of his time. I don't know where I'd be if he hadn't helped me over some very rough times spiritually and helped me with my marriage also. Even though my husband is a Christian, he's not living it much of the time, and I don't feel nearly as free talking to him as I do to my pastor. We have real *rapport,* and I have also been used by the Holy Spirit to minister to his needs many times. My neighbor tells me I am wrong, and that I'm using my pastor as a sort of substitute husband. She says that I'm being unfair to my husband, my pastor, and also my pastor's wife. I feel that as long as my pastor can help me better than my husband can, I should continue to go to him. Do you agree?

Dear Endangered,

You may be walking into or unknowingly creating an enticing trap. It is doubtful whether any man and woman who are continually together, especially if they are sharing about personal things, can maintain what is sometimes called a platonic relationship. When we hear of a pastor who has left his wife in favor of his secretary, or his choir directress, we may think it strange that a man of God would take such a tumble, yet the basic reason is simple—they were together

too often. Too many homes have been broken up by relationships which seemed innocent at first. Watch out for
those so-called innocent beginnings. As Paul advised the
Thessalonians, avoid the very appearance of evil (1 Thessalonians 5:22).

If you need to talk with your minister confidentially, do so
at his office, with his secretary nearby. Private counseling
sessions at your home or in other secluded situations can be
an open invitation to problems. If you need to consult with
him frequently, why don't you ask if you can talk with him
at his house with his wife present? Ask yourself, "Do I still
want his advice if I have to have his wife there?" Any long-
continued counseling situation between a man and woman is
not wise. It's never advisable for men and women to minister to one another in private, unless, of course, they are
married, or engaged, or family members. We always recommend that, wherever possible, counseling be done by two
people counseling one. Especially where a man is counseling
a woman, or vice versa, another counselor should be present. You may think you and your pastor are completely
above being misled, but don't be deceived—the flesh is
weak. Spiritual attachment moves over so quickly to psychological and physical attachment.

Gifts of the Holy Spirit such as prophecy and knowledge
should not be used in such a way as to make another person's husband dependent on you.

Avoid Further Complications

Even if you're sure your motives are pure, please take this
advice: avoid further complications. Have you ever thought
of talking to a reliable Christian woman with some knowledge of counseling? This would be much safer. An increasing number of churches and individuals are getting involved
in prayer counseling for soul healing, or inner healing. Have

you looked into this? May I suggest that you get some of the many good books on this subject. (*See* chapter 17.)

It would be surprising if your closeness to your pastor is not causing your husband to feel competition. This could drive him further away from you and the Lord. I once heard it put this way: "Your husband will not cherish you if you are letting another man do the cherishing." If you find after breaking up this close fellowship with your pastor, that you miss it more than you should, it might be best for you and your husband to move to another church.

Many good people have been warned in time, and awakened before they went too far in a wrong relationship. You can thank your neighbor for being honest enough to warn you. Others may have felt the same way, but lacked the courage to talk to you about it. May God bless and guide you and keep you in the center of His love and will.

26

How Can I Stop Seeing Red?

Dear Rita,

I have had a quick temper most of my life. In the past, I've always excused it on the grounds that I have red hair! I have come to realize I can't go on blaming my temper on the color of my hair! After being undisciplined in this area most of my life, what can I do now to help myself, and my husband and family, too?

Dear Redhead,

You've often been told, I'm sure, "If you're mad at someone, count to ten before you say anything." Recently I heard something better. "If you are really angry, count to nine by naming the nine fruits of the Holy Spirit!"

A short time after I heard this, something happened to get me stirred up, so I thought, *I'll just count to nine.* I started counting with the first fruit, love, and that's as far as I needed to count. With the remembrance of the forgiving love of God toward me and everyone else, I couldn't hold a grudge.

Memorize the fruit of the Spirit so you, too, can count to nine: love, joy, peace, patience, kindness, goodness, faithfulness, humility, discipline (Galatians 5:22, 23, author's paraphrase). It's interesting that the ninth fruit is discipline (self-control), which you especially expressed your need for.

I'm glad to hear that the old wives' tale about red hair has been exposed by the Holy Spirit. The enemy of our souls enjoys giving reasons for our sins, so we will excuse them, keeping them as seemingly harmless pets, rather than getting rid of them. Having a bad temper is like harboring a wild beast in your backyard. You can either keep feeding him three square meals a day, you can give him a bare daily ration, or you can stop feeding him altogether. This third choice is, I'm sure, what you have in mind.

Did Jesus Lose His Temper?

Jesus Christ may have had red hair, at least that's how Flavius Josephus, a Jewish historian living in the first century, described Him. Can you imagine Jesus losing His temper, and using red hair for an excuse! Only once does the New Testament say that Jesus was angry. The Pharisees were watching Him closely to see if He would break the Law by healing on the Sabbath, so they would have something on Him. Before healing the man, Jesus asked, "Is it lawful to do good on the sabbath day, or to do evil? . . ." (Mark 3:4). But they wouldn't answer Him. He then looked at them "with anger, being grieved for the hardness of their hearts . . ." (Mark 3:5). Jesus looked into their souls and was angered at the work of His ancient enemy, Satan, within these men.

Another place where Jesus expressed anger (although the word isn't used) was when He found the priests and scribes sponsoring the sale of sacrificial animals in the Temple and making a large profit thereby. He dumped over the tables and chased the men out (Matthew 21:12, 13). This was the only kind of anger Jesus had: anger with the enemy and His co-workers. He did not get angry over wrongs done to Himself. Jesus did not "lose His temper" because He was in control of Himself, and knew exactly what He was doing at all times.

One can think of numerous places in the Scriptures where Jesus was badly treated, and yet responded with gentleness and love. Even while He was being nailed to the cross unjustly, Jesus was praying that His Father would forgive those who were doing it. He was certainly not the "angry young man" that some try to portray Him.

"Be Angry, and Do Not Sin"

The Apostle Paul wrote to his friends in Ephesus, "If you're angry, do not sin: don't let the sun set while you're still angry: don't give any place to the devil" (*see* Ephesians 4:26, 27). Apparently it is possible to be angry without sinning, but we must not allow the devil to turn it into hatred or to use it for his purposes, nor must we hold on to it and let it smolder in our hearts. It's good to get the anger out in appropriate ways, such as through talking it out with someone and then praying; or, if alone, talking it out with God in prayer.

This is a verse my husband and I have put into practice from the first of our marriage. If one of us has said or done something hurtful (most often unknowingly), neither of us can go to sleep until we've talked it out, asked forgiveness, and have prayed about it—even if it's one o'clock in the morning. This way the enemy cannot get a wedge between us, which he would then try to enlarge. I highly recommend the application of this verse to your life.

Jesus taught that the things we put into our mouths do not defile our souls but what comes out of our mouths will (Matthew 15:17, 18). Bad temper and angry words will defile us if not handled properly. We can pray as the psalmist did: "Set a watch, O Lord, before my mouth; keep the door of my lips" (Psalms 141:3).

James warns, ". . . Let every man be quick to hear, slow to speak, slow to anger, for the anger of man does not work the righteousness of God" (James 1:19 RSV). That's good advice, isn't it? "Quick to hear" and "slow to speak."

Next time you need help and after you've counted to nine, you might try praying "in the Spirit" (*see* 1 Corinthians 14:14, 15) for a little while. That should cool your anger down a bit. After praying for God's help, when you do speak, I believe your words will be full of love and joy.

Honestly facing your need, and sincerely wanting to change, are two of the first steps in receiving God's help. Since you've already taken these steps, the rest will surely follow.

27

Can You Help Me Kick the
Smoking Habit?

Dear Rita,

I recently rededicated my life to God, but I still can't quit smoking. My husband had no problem giving it up. I guess he's stronger, or more obedient than I am. What can I do about it?

Dear Smoker,

First of all, don't let your smoking stand between you and the Lord. Smoking is a harmful habit, but it isn't the first deadly sin—which is what many Christians seem to make it. My husband, Dennis, and I boarded a flight from Chicago to Minneapolis several years ago. When flying commercially, we generally pray and ask God to give us a person to witness to. As we walked down the aisle, we found that we were assigned seats next to a blind man, probably in his early fifties. Tall, with a pleasant face, he toyed absentmindedly with his white cane. Dennis took the seat next to him and I sat next to the aisle.

In a short time, Dennis and his neighbor were in conversation. The man was from a Pentecostal background, and not only that, his father was a minister. When Dennis asked if he was a Christian, the man replied, "Oh, no, I've never been able to give up cigarettes." We were both startled by his answer, as we realized his misconception of what it meant to be a Christian was actually keeping him from accepting Jesus. Dennis talked with him further, and led him to pray to receive Jesus as his Savior. I sat praying quietly and rejoicing. As our new Christian brother was getting off the airplane, he told us that the recorder he was carrying had a tape of the Gospel of John on it, which he had just received that week but hadn't listened to yet! The Lord had surely set the stage for our visit with him, and as he listened to the Scriptures, I'm sure they came alive for him.

Did he quit smoking? We don't know. I heard this quoted years ago, "God catches His fish before He cleans them." I'm sure God helped him deal with his smoking, and no doubt with other more serious problems.

A young man with a bad smoking habit (and a background of being condemned for it) was seated on an airplane next to a well-known singer and evangelist. After chatting a bit, the young man said, "Say, Tony, can I smoke cigarettes and still go to heaven?" Tony thought a moment and replied, "Why, yes!" Then he added, with a smile, "And you'll get there a whole lot faster, too!"

No Condemnation

Don't condemn yourself, or let yourself be condemned because you have not yet been able to stop smoking, and don't think that God rejects you because of it. The reasons to stop are not so much spiritual as practical. It's harmful to your health, a waste of money, a nuisance, a possible hazard, and it certainly does not increase your feminine attractiveness!

There are many reasons why people smoke. Psychologists say causes for the habit can be traced back to an infant's unsatisfied need to be held and loved by her mother. The cigarette is like a pacifier, giving oral satisfaction. The picture of a woman with a pacifier in her mouth certainly isn't appealing, but, in fact, that may be what smoking means to you subconsciously.

Some started smoking as youngsters because they were told it was evil. Being rebellious, they just naturally wanted to try it! It was a way to hit back at parents and assert one's independence.

Some people smoke because they think it sophisticated, and want to be accepted by friends they admire who smoke. There is a kind of fellowship in smoking. It's something to do together. "You light my cigarette, and I'll light yours." Advertising has done much to get this idea across.

Insecure people may feel important and on top of things when they're smoking. They may feel awkward or self-conscious and not know what else to do with their hands, so they smoke.

People also smoke because they don't have the willpower to curb their eating, so take up smoking as a substitute. Smoking dulls the taste buds, so that food doesn't have as much appeal.

Many people are just plain bored. Those with occupations like long-distance truck driving, or other vocations where they spend much time alone, performing a routine task, can be tempted to fill the gap by smoking. The same is true of those in the armed forces.

As for your battle in trying to give up smoking, I know what you're talking about, although I was a smoker for only five years or so. Looking back on it now, I realize one of the reasons I smoked was I was rebelling against my religious background; it was believed to be one of the Top Ten sins! Also, I smoked because I wanted to be "with it" and accepted by my peer group. Then, too, I was curious to know why so many people liked to smoke.

I met the Lord when I was a child, but I walked away from Him for a number of years. In my twenties, I began to return to the faith of my childhood. One day I realized, while praying in church, that I was thinking about my next cigarette, rather than about God. This made me think: was I going to put God in second place to this habit the rest of my life? A short time later, just before I was released in the power of the Holy Spirit, I prayed, "Dear Father, if You want me to give up smoking, please take the desire for cigarettes away from me." Then I added, "If You do this, Lord, I will never smoke again." The empowering of the Holy Spirit, shortly after this prayer, met the inner needs of which smoking was an outward symptom, and I haven't smoked since that day in 1960. I now think too much of myself (Jesus taught me to love myself) to shorten my life through this habit.

A Spirit of Self-Destruction?

I believe there is a spirit of self-destruction that urges a person to keep on smoking, even when he or she wants to stop. I remember smoking a number of times, even when I had tonsilitis and a raw throat, or a bad cold. I have a lovely friend who has emphysema, and yet continues to make her condition worse by smoking. Another friend, who was in social work, had to have a lung removed, but continued to smoke, even at times when she was having trouble breathing. She died at an early age. It reminds me of the Scripture describing Satan saying, "The thief cometh not, but for to steal, and to kill, and to destroy . . ." (John 10:10). Continuous smoking can take years off a person's life, as the medical warnings these days bear proof.

Some Christians, because they do not find chapter and verse in the Bible against smoking, think that's an excuse to smoke. They want to find an additional commandment which says, "Thou shalt not smoke." But the Old Testament promises that God will come to dwell in people, and the New Testament says that promise is fulfilled in those who have received Christ. They have become temples of the Holy Spirit. "What? Don't you know that your body is the temple of the Holy Ghost which is in you, which you have of God, and you are not your own? For you are bought with a price: therefore glorify God in your body . . ." (1 Corinthians 6:19, 20, author's paraphrase). (It wouldn't be fair, of course, to aim this Scripture entirely at smoking. It would apply to any habit that mistreats the body, including overeating, or overdrinking, drinking excessive amounts of coffee or tea, taking drugs, and so forth.)

A person who cannot control his smoking often has a deep need for healing in his life. As that inner need is met, and the hurt healed, the person no longer needs to smoke. You received much healing when you received Jesus as Savior, and when you rededicated your life to Christ. Every experience with Jesus brings soul healing. There may, however, be hidden hurts in your soul which the Lord has not yet been able to reach. You may need to find a person who understands prayer for inner or soul healing, and let him or her work with you.

Fourteen Ways to Kick the Smoking Habit

Let me then list some of the things I believe may help you and others kick the smoking habit:

1. Meet Jesus as Savior.

2. Be baptized in the Holy Spirit.

3. Consecrate your life to Jesus; present your body to Him.

4. Spend fifteen minutes or more each day in prayer and reading Scripture and other helpful books on spiritual life.

5. Pray for healing of your soul, your emotions, and memories.

6. If you had a traumatic birth, or lacked normal feeding and holding right after birth and those months following, seek prayer help from someone experienced in inner healing.

7. Forgive everyone, and know that God has forgiven you.

8. Receive prayer for deliverance.

9. Check on your dietary habits. If you give your body the nutrients it needs, perhaps the craving for cigarettes will lessen.

10. You might well see one of the movies that show what happens to the lungs of a heavy smoker! You can probably see such a film at one of the clinics some churches offer to those wanting to quit smoking. It might be a good idea to attend a clinic like this.

11. Limit contacts with old smoking buddies who still smoke up a storm! At least until you're stronger, choose new friends who don't smoke.

12. Call a nonsmoking Christian friend when you are tempted to smoke, and ask him or her to talk to you and pray with you to help you through withdrawal.

13. Figure out how much money is wasted on cigarettes each year, including clothes you've burnt holes in. Plan something worthwhile to do with the money you save.

14. Start a program of physical exercise; teach yourself discipline in this way. You'll probably find that jogging and smoking don't go together.

The answer to your letter turned out to be an epistle!

While you're working on this problem, remember again, God loves you right now—just as you are. Don't let frustration or condemnation come into your life; they will just send you in the wrong direction. At the same time, remember God has a wonderful plan for you, which you can interfere with by throwing away years of priceless life in this harmful pastime.

Concentrate on how much God loves you, and then love Him back with all your might. You'll soon kick that smoking habit right out of your life!

28

I'm in Love With My Pastor—
What Shall I Do?

Dear Rita,

Please don't quote my name if you use this question, because I wouldn't want anyone to know about my situation. For the past year, I have been in love with my pastor. (I am single.) Even though he's married to a nice wife and has several children, and though he has never said so, I know he feels the same way about me. On Sundays, I hardly hear the sermon, because all I can think of is this man. I try to put these thoughts out of my mind, but in a few minutes, they are back stronger than ever. I take part in every church activity, so I can be where he is, even though I know I shouldn't. Should I go to him and tell him how I feel and ask his advice? Please help me, but don't ask me to change churches. My family has been part of this church for three generations, and I could never explain if I wanted to quit going there.

Dear In-Love-With-the-Pastor,

What does it mean to be *in love?* As I see it, love is caring about another person more than you do yourself, or anyone else in this world. It's not wanting to hurt that person in any way. It's helping that person be fulfilled in spirit, soul, and body, and desiring his love for God to grow beyond all loves. True love would not do anything to come between a person and God. It wants God's first best for that person's life and works to that end. When a Christian has found the right person to spend his or her earthly life with, God will confirm this to his or her spirit, and it will be in agreement with the Scripture.

Isn't it obvious that loving and desiring a married man—and pursuing him—is against everything that truly is love? You've been living in fantasy, but let's face it—the direction you are going could ultimately lead to breaking apart a family!

You've asked for help, so here goes. First of all, you must determine in your own heart that the way you've been headed is wrong. Next, stop taking part in extra church activities where your pastor will be present. You may feel you have to continue to attend your own church on Sunday morning, but find another church, Bible study or prayer group where you can be spiritually fed during the week. For a year, the enemy has stolen your spiritual food by making your ears deaf to what God wanted to say to you, and therefore making you more open to Satan's suggestions. James 1:14, 15 says: "But each one is tempted when he is drawn away by his own desires and enticed. Then, when desire has conceived, it gives birth to sin; and sin, when it is full-grown, brings forth death" (NKJB).

I don't think you should talk about your feelings with your pastor. If he is personally drawn to you, talking to him might increase the temptation in his own life and lead to trouble. If it is all on your part, it would be a great embarrassment to you both, and to you in particular.

Pastors have to realize that unhappily married or single women who admire them, especially those to whom they have ministered in counseling and prayer, can mistake the love of God for human love. This may happen even in situations where there has been very little contact.

Receive Soul-Healing Prayer

If, after taking the steps I have recommended, you are still having serious trouble controlling your thought life, you may need prayer for healing of past hurts in your soul that are causing you to have uncontrollable needs. You should read books on inner healing and seek prayer help from those who are experienced in this kind of prayer.

The Lord has the right man for you to marry, but you are making it impossible for this to come to pass by living in a fantasy world. Your future depends on what you put into your life today. Just as the farmer has a choice about the seeds he sows into the ground, so we have a choice about the seed thoughts we put into our lives. One of the greatest powers we have is to choose what we will think about. We act upon what we think, and we will eventually reap what we sow in the field of our minds.

A Scripture that has helped me to have a victorious thought life is, "Casting down imaginations, and every high thing that exalteth itself against the knowledge of God, and bringing into captivity every thought to the obedience of Christ" (2 Corinthians 10:5). With this Scripture, I picture Jesus capturing my unworthy thoughts and setting me free.

The mind is a real battleground. Your mind has been bombarded by wrong thoughts for a year, which though you did not act upon, you entertained and so tempted yourself—and the thoughts remained. When you yield territory to the enemy, he doesn't give it up without a fight. It is going to take some effort on your part, but Jesus is on your side, and that ground will be regained.

29

Why Do I Feel Guilty?

Dear Rita,

I'm a Christian, but I have a recurring feeling that I have committed what the Bible calls the unpardonable sin. I often feel guilty, condemned, and actually unredeemed. I need help!

I will give you some background. I awoke at the age of seven, at a revival meeting, in time to hear about the unpardonable sin and to hear the preacher say, "If you don't want to go to hell, step forward." I stepped forward. I don't remember praying to receive Jesus Christ at all. I was a sinful little kid and grew up to be a sinful big kid.

I was married in my teenage years and began having children during the time my husband was working and going to the university. All this added pressure to my life, and several years after our marriage, I awoke one night "feeling" lost, condemned. After several weeks of torment, my pastor and I were praying at the church and the burden lifted. I "felt" the glory of the Lord, and for a couple of days I thought, and claimed, this as my saving experience and was baptized in a nearby river.

I fell away, however, became involved in some flagrant sinning, and everything began to fall apart. Unhappy, I erroneously thought the Lord had let me down and began a heathen life for a number of years. My sins were gross, involving addiction to alcohol, and adultery that followed drunkenness. My husband forgave me after I confessed all to him. In 1969, at a revival meeting, I made a hand-raising recommitment to the Lord, and then tried honestly to turn away from sin. A year later, following a party where I had one too many, I asked the Lord to come into my life, based on Revelation 3:20. I believed I had made peace with the Lord, but didn't tell anyone about this, except with a changed life (which I really tried to change). Lately I have been having doubts and losing interest in witnessing, although I believe I have led several people to the Lord.

At any rate, I thought I received the Baptism with the Holy Spirit, and was on Cloud Nine. A week later, I became burdened but didn't know why. Then, **Boom!** I was filled with depression, guilt, condemnation, confusion, and a feeling of lostness.

I'm in a mess. Could you shed some light on my problem? I have been telling myself to trust Him regardless of how I feel, but I should be Spirit-filled and happy instead of depressed and feeling condemned. I have once again thought that I must have committed the unpardonable sin. Can you help me? Please?

Dear In-Need,

From what I can see from your letter, you have had guilt and condemnation heaped on your head from the very beginning. As a result you rebelled; because the rules imposed on you were so rigid, it was impossible to keep them. Apparently you also absorbed the idea that every time you sin, God leaves you.

But Scripture says about Jesus, "... For He has said, I will never, never leave you, and I will not, I will not, I will not forsake you" (Hebrews 13:5, author's paraphrase). This is the way the literal Greek reads. Once we've invited Jesus in, He does not leave us. We may feel that He has left us, because sin separates us from the sense of His presence, but when we put things right, the relationship is reestablished immediately. Jesus hasn't left us—we have left Him!

Here is the pattern: you committed some small offense; then, because you thought God had left you, communication broke down. If God was gone, all seemed to be lost anyway, so you thought you might as well accept the next suggestion of the tempter, and thus you went further into wrongdoing. In this way, your life got more and more torn up. The enemy had a heyday messing up a temple of the Holy Spirit. Then you heard an evangelist, got reconvicted, and dedicated your life over again, but you did not know how to receive the power of the Holy Spirit. You undoubtedly went through this painful process many times.

Some ministers, knowing only the doctrines of sin, hell, and salvation, keep people coming to church through fear. These are, of course, basic teachings—although they are not meant to be taught in the way you apparently heard them. God is not eager to send people to hell. Hell is the destination of those who finally refuse God's every effort to bring them to Himself. But there is more to Christianity than this. Hebrews 6:1 says, "Therefore, leaving the beginning principles of the doctrine of Christ let us go on" (author's paraphrase). If you don't move on with Christ, you will be likely to lose much of the progress you have made. Hebrews doesn't say we should give up the basic doctrines, but that we should go on and build on them.

You have not committed the unpardonable sin. If you had, you would have no interest in or desire for Jesus—your heart would be totally hardened against God. That, obviously, isn't your case. We believe this Scripture (Matthew 12:32) doesn't refer to believers at all, but of those who harden their hearts against Jesus each time the Holy Spirit invites them to receive Him, until they become totally immune. If a person could look at the things Jesus did and attribute them to the devil, and continue to do so throughout his lifetime, that person could never become a true believer in Christ, could he? *This* is the unforgivable sin, refusing to accept God's offer of Himself through Jesus Christ. This sin is unpardonable because the person has no desire to ask for pardon. In other words, the sin is unforgiv*able,* not *able* to be forgiven, because forgiveness is neither asked for nor received.

God's Unconditional Love Heals

You may have picked up this irrational fear of committing the unpardonable sin from some of the sermons you heard in your youth. Those frightening thoughts are also lodged in your subconscious mind, and need to be dealt with there. That frightened little girl of the past is still a part of you. She needs to be healed. Through prayer, see Jesus there with you in that scene in your childhood, and let His unconditional love melt away the fear. You might want to have a friend help you pray through this memory in more detail. You will be surprised at what will happen as you allow Jesus to fix up your past feelings. Forgive those who frightened you, realizing they were doing the best they knew how at the time.

The enemy has drawn on old memories to condemn you. Remember, it is Satan who condemns, but the Holy Spirit *convicts*; that is, He makes us realize that we are wrong, so that we will do something about it. The devil says, "You're no good, and never will be." The Holy Spirit says, "God loves you, and so He wants you to straighten up and fly right!" The Holy Spirit is specific. He doesn't leave us with a vague feeling of guilt for we know not what. A great Scripture for you to think about is, "There is therefore now no condemnation to them which are in Christ Jesus, who walk not after the flesh, but after the Spirit" (Romans 8:1).

If you remember fear-producing statements spoken by ministers or parents in your childhood, which the enemy is *still* using to condemn you, then by a conscious act of your will, refuse that condemnation in Jesus' Name.

Have you seen the book (co-authored with my husband, Dennis) *The Holy Spirit and You*? The chapter on discerning of spirits tells about casting away the influence of the enemy. Your fearful memories are like fiery darts, which can be resisted and cast away in Jesus' Name. You can pray something like this: "Spirit of condemnation, I bind you in the Name of Jesus and under His precious blood. I cast you away from me in Jesus' Name!" Do this with each troubling thought you are aware of. Here's a suggested list: spirit of condemnation; spirit of unbelief; lying spirit; tormenting spirit; spirit of depression; spirit of guilt; deceiving spirit; spirit of confusion; and anything else the Holy Spirit shows you. You may want to pray alone or with someone else. Don't spend *too* much time in this activity. The Bible says to be ". . . simple concerning evil" (Romans 16:19). Know that you have authority over the enemy. Resist him, and he must flee. Then ask God's Holy Spirit to fill you, and try to keep your life centered in Jesus.

Difference Between Soul and Spirit

I would recommend that you get a copy of Watchman Nee's *Release of the Spirit,* and also *Trinity of Man,* by Dennis and me. You need to understand the difference between your soul (*psyche*) and spirit (*pneuma*), in order to understand what has happened to you in the past and to know how to cope with your present situation. When you were feeling on Cloud Nine, all was well with you and God; your regenerated spirit was in control. When you began to doubt and felt condemned again, your soul was getting back on top. Your emotions or feelings are from your soul, and cannot be relied on to guide your life.

Since you walked away from God and established bad habit patterns over a period of time, you will naturally have greater battles for a while after you return to the Lord, and the battle will especially be in the area of the mind. As you are healed, you will more and more be able to cast out thoughts that contradict God, and get your mind back on that which is good and true.

Suggestions to Help You Win This Battle

Have frequent fellowship with like-minded believers, and pray in the Spirit often. You will find the battle growing less difficult, and will find yourself walking in a greater awareness of the Holy Spirit.

Get a concordance and go through the Bible, writing down every Scripture that confirms your salvation, and that shows God has removed your sins (such as, Psalms 103:10–17; Isaiah 1:18; 1 John 1:7, 9; 5:11–15). You might copy such Scriptures for easy reference, and read them each day before you pray. Listen to good tapes with positive messages, and go to church where the minister speaks life, not condemnation. This will be healing to you.

You have invited Jesus to come into your life; you have confessed your sins and have no doubt put things right where possible; the Holy Spirit has blessed your life recently. God loves you! If you will do the other things mentioned in this letter, as the Holy Spirit guides, you are bound to have victory. God has begun a good work in your life, and He always completes what He begins.

On the back of a sand and gravel truck, I once saw a sign which read FIND A NEED AND FILL IT. The thought came to me that that's exactly what God does. He will fill your every need with the power of His presence and His love. Then you can be like the fellow in the truck (your truck will be full of God's healing love, instead of sand and gravel!); after having your own needs met, you'll be able to fill up the emptiness in other people's lives. That's when things will really get exciting. And that's exactly what God has in store for you!

SPIRITUAL
LIFE

30

How Can I Prepare to Witness?

Dear Rita,

Recently, while visiting an old friend in Florida, I was challenged by her husband, who claims to be an atheist. He told me that Jesus never claimed to be God incarnate; that Jesus was only a man like anyone else. I didn't know what to say to him, so I gave him a terribly inadequate answer, which I know did not help him. I feel bad about this and guess I really failed in witnessing. What could I have said?

Dear Failure-in-Witnessing,

Every one of us is a failure at times, but God can turn every failure into a positive learning experience. Without the unsatisfactory confrontation with your friend's husband, you would not have been challenged to find out what you didn't know.

When I was speaking at a Christian women's luncheon in Victoria, B.C., around the year 1967, I, too, was challenged. A woman present kept ordering cocktail after cocktail from the bar, while sitting at a table with the rest of the group. Obviously she had a problem, and the other women didn't know exactly what to do about it.

After the meeting, while I was praying with people, I received word that someone in the hotel bar and lounge wanted to speak to me. When I arrived I found it was the same woman I had noticed in the meeting. She must have slipped out near the end.

Like your friend's husband, she challenged me to prove that Jesus is God. I found, sad to say, that I didn't have as much ammunition as I needed, but I did tell her that she didn't so much need to know intellectually that Jesus is God, as to experience Him. If she really wanted to know who He was, she needed to ask Him to show her His love, and heal her life. I talked and prayed with her, and I trust she was helped. I'm sure it would have been better, though, if I could have given her more from the Scriptures.

As soon as I returned home, I made quite a study and wrote the pertinent Scriptures on the subject in the back of my small Bible. As I studied, I found that Jesus most often spoke of Himself as the "Son of man," identifying Himself with humanity. He didn't often speak of His divinity, or try to show that He was God. He knew it was necessary for others to recognize Him first as the Father revealed it to them through the Holy Spirit. For example, Matthew tells how one day Jesus asked His disciples, "Who do men say that I, the Son of man, am?" Or, to put it in the vernacular, "What are people saying about Me nowadays?" "So they said, Some say you are John the Baptist, some Elijah, and others Jeremiah or one of the prophets" (Matthew 16:13, 14 NKJB).

Jesus' Divinity

Then Jesus asked a more personal question that everyone has to answer, "But who do you say that I am?" Simon Peter came through with flying colors! "You are the Christ," he said, "the Son of the living God." Jesus was delighted with Peter's answer. "Blessed are you, Simon Bar-Jonah," He said, "for flesh and blood has not revealed this to you, but My Father who is in heaven" (Matthew 16:15–17, both NKJB).

As soon as Peter made his confession that Jesus is the Christ, Jesus confirmed it, but He wanted it to come from Peter. Jesus clearly admits here that He is the Son of God, and the Christ, the Anointed Messiah of God. Nathanael confessed the same thing, and Jesus accepted it (John 1:47–51).

Jesus did sometimes clearly claim or give evidence of His divinity. The Gospel of John has more about it than the others. In John 8, a significant debate is recorded between the unbelieving Jews and Jesus. Jesus is claiming that whoever believes on Him will never see death. He goes on to say, "Your father Abraham rejoiced to see my day: and he saw it, and was glad" (John 8:56). This puzzled the Jews, who realized Jesus was a young man, while Abraham had been dead for some two thousand years. Jesus then said words which threw them into a rage: "I assure you . . . before Abraham was born, I AM" (John 8:58 AMPLIFIED). Here Jesus used the ancient Hebrew name of God which was thought to be so sacred it was never uttered. Remember, when Moses asked God His Name at the burning bush (Exodus 3:13, 14) God replied, "Thus shalt thou say unto the children of Israel, I AM hath sent me unto you." The Jews took Jesus' statement as a claim to be God, or they wouldn't have tried to kill Him.

Jesus often said to people, "Your sins are forgiven." Long before He was raised from the dead Himself, He did not hesitate to say, "I am the resurrection, and the life . . ." (John 11:25). He admitted to the woman at the well that He was the promised Messiah, the Anointed One. Other spiritual leaders claimed to teach the truth, but Jesus claimed to *be* the truth, and life itself. Others claimed to show the way, but

Jesus said, "I am the way." He said, ". . . no man cometh unto the Father, but by me" (John 14:6). He said, ". . . I am the light of the world . . ." (John 8:12). On the Mount of Transfiguration, His face shone so brightly that Peter, James, and John couldn't look at Him.

When the soldiers came to the Garden of Gethsemane looking for Jesus to imprison and crucify Him, they didn't recognize Him. They asked which one was Jesus of Nazareth, and Jesus in His answer again used the words, "I AM!" There was such power in that Name the soldiers all fell over backwards on the ground (John 18:6)! (When a word is in italics in KJV, that means it wasn't in the original manuscript but was added by the translators. So when it says, "I am he," it would actually read, "I am.")

When Jesus appeared before the high priest, he badgered Him for not defending Himself, and asked Him, ". . . Are you the Christ—the Messiah, the Anointed One—the Son of the Blessed?" Jesus' reply made His Crucifixion certain. Once more He used the great Name. He said, "I AM; and you will (all) see the Son of man seated at the right hand of Power (the Almighty), and coming with the clouds of heaven" (Mark 14:61, 62 AMPLIFIED). The high priest tore his garments, cried "Blasphemy!" and condemned Jesus. It's obvious here again that he realized Jesus was claiming to be divine.

Finally, in John 20:24–31, you'll find it clearest of all. The other disciples had seen Jesus after His Resurrection, but "doubting" Thomas wasn't with them. When he heard the news, he said, "Unless I am able to see and touch the scars in His hands and put my hand into the spear wound in His side, I won't believe." Eight days later, Jesus visited the disciples again, and this time Thomas was there. Knowing what Thomas had said, Jesus showed him His hands and side. Thomas said simply, "My Lord and my God!" Jesus

didn't say, "Oh, no, Thomas, I'm just a man like you," He
accepted Thomas's acknowledgment of Him as God and His
worship of Him.

An Important Prayer

There are other passages in the Epistles and Old Testament as well as the Gospels which you can look up yourself,
but if you mark these major ones in your Bible, you'll be
better prepared next time. You could write to your friend's
husband and share these Scriptures with him. Remember,
however, he'll never intellectualize his way to God. It's not
wrong for him to ask questions, of course, but after they're
answered, he still must receive Jesus in faith before he can
know who He is.

It's all right to be completely honest with God. I once
heard of a man who prayed: "Oh, God, if there is a God,
save my soul if I have a soul!" I'm sure if such a prayer were
sincerely made, God would answer it.

Ask your friend to try an experiment and say, "God, if
You are real, and if Jesus is Your Son, I invite Him to come
into my life and make Himself real to me. Thank You."
God will answer a prayer like this, so be prepared to hear
further from your friend's husband.

31

How Can a Mother Find
Time to Pray?

Dear Rita,

I'm in my early twenties, married, and have three children under five. It troubles me that I never have time to pray like most of the people in my church. Several of my friends get up before their families do and spend an hour in prayer and Bible study. They have prayer lists, and they pray faithfully for all the people on them. Just hearing about their schedules makes me feel very unspiritual. Am I fooling myself when I say this is an impossible goal for me? How much time should I be taking to pray?

Dear Feeling Unspiritual,

I saw this motto recently: LIFE IS FRAGILE, HANDLE WITH PRAYER. That would be a good thing to stick on the bumper of the car, a suitcase, or packages that need special handling. It would be good if we could somehow stick it onto our lives!

Prayer is talking with God, communicating love and need—for yourself and others. It's also listening to God talk to you, giving you encouragement and direction. It is the breath of life to anyone who knows God, because He created us to be His friends.

Therefore, it shouldn't be such hard work. Often, the way people talk about prayer, they make it seem impossible for

any but those who have withdrawn into a monastery or a
convent to be real people of prayer. A prayer list, too, can be
a helpful reminder, but it's possible to read such a list me-
chanically, without following the Lord's leading, or enjoy-
ing His presence.

It's a good idea to have a set time each day to devote to
prayer and Scripture reading. Don't start with a long period,
but aim at fifteen minutes at first. You can then lengthen it
as you feel ready to. If that time is interrupted by the demands of the family, you can still talk to God through the
day. He's always there! You'll hear Christians talk about
"coming before the Lord," or "entering the throne room,"
or something like that, which may subtly get across the notion that we have to make a formal approach to God in
order to speak to Him. But the Good News is, "The Kingdom of Heaven is at hand. God is here. He is available!"

Prayer in a Busy Life

There's a place for reading "formal" prayers, but informal, spontaneous praying you can do anytime. Try talking
to the Lord while you clean house, wash dishes, iron clothes,
or drive to the grocery store. If you prayed at every opportunity like this, even in your busy life, you would probably
find you're praying as much as your friends, or perhaps
more!

Praying in the course of a busy schedule wasn't easy for
me, nor did I spend much time at it, until I received the
power of the Holy Spirit. At that time, I discovered a new
way to pray. I began to praise God and talk to Him in a language given to me by the Holy Spirit. This is what the Bible
calls praying in the Spirit. Paul says, "For if I pray in a
tongue, my spirit prays, but my understanding is unfruitful.
What is the result then? I will pray with the spirit, and I will
also pray with the understanding. I will sing with the spirit,

and I will also sing with the understanding" (1 Corinthians 14:14, 15 NKJB).

Praying in the Spirit means trusting God to give you words with which you can pray beyond the limitations of your intellect. When we run out of our own words with which to communicate to God, we can just open our mouths and trust Him to give us the words He wants us to say. This is a most refreshing way to pray, in addition to praying in your own language. Since you won't have to think about what you're saying when you pray this way, you can easily be doing household tasks and other things at the same time. You can also sing in the Spirit, letting the Holy Spirit guide both the words and music, giving you a brand-new song.

So if you haven't begun to use this prayer in the Spirit, do so. It's just as easy as accepting Jesus. As mentioned earlier, our book *The Holy Spirit and You* gives detailed instructions how to prepare and pray for it. If you know Christians who understand about this, and will pray with you, so much the better; but you can receive this release of the Holy Spirit by yourself, if necessary. Many do.

Praying in the Spirit doesn't just refer to speaking in tongues. Any sincere prayer, in whatever language, is prayer in the Spirit, for it is only by the spirit (that innermost part of us where God comes to live when we receive Jesus) that we can contact God at all. However, the more freely you pray in the Spirit—the more you will be refreshed and you will feel like praying more.

How Much Time?

How much time should you spend? The Bible says we're supposed to be referring our lives to God at all times! "Praying always with all prayer and supplication in the Spirit ..." (Ephesians 6:18); "Pray without ceasing" (1 Thessalonians 5:17); "... in every thing by prayer and sup-

plication with thanksgiving let your requests be made
known unto God" (Philippians 4:6). Informal, conversa-
tional prayer, and prayer in the Spirit make this possible.

I believe that even when you're asleep, your spirit is praying. It might be good to pray before going to bed, "Lord,
while I rest, I want my spirit to be in communication and
fellowship with You." This may sound awfully easy, just
lying there in bed, expecting your spirit to do the work! But
sometimes God will call you to attention, and ask you to
pray for some special need for another person, which takes
more effort.

Basically speaking, though, prayer should be as easy as
breathing. As the psalmist, David, says, "Let every thing that
hath breath praise the Lord . . ." (Psalms 150:6). If you're
breathing, then you should be praying and praising God.

32

Is It Possible for Children to Understand Spiritual Matters?

Dear Rita,

One of my children, a little girl, five years old, is asking a lot of questions about Jesus. She seems especially interested in the Crucifixion, and wants me to read her that story from our Bible storybook over and over. It seems to make her sad, but she loves it just the same. Is this normal? What should I tell her about the Lord?

Dear Mother,

Little children are much more ready to hear and understand about God our Father, and about Jesus Christ and what He did for us, than we imagine they are. It is not at all unusual for very young children to take a deep interest in spiritual things, and especially to be fascinated by Jesus and everything about Him, including His Crucifixion. Somehow, they seem instinctively to know the importance of it. It is surprising the grasp young children sometimes have of deep theological matters.

While my husband and I were holding a mission in the Episcopal Cathedral in Jacksonville, Florida, several years ago, a sweet little six-year-old girl, the daughter of one of the leading laymen, came to me. This youngster had already received Jesus as her Savior and been baptized in the Holy Spirit; now she was telling her playmates about Jesus.

She brought with her a five-year-old friend, whom she had told about Jesus; but she had a question! "Mrs. Bennett, please explain the Trinity to me." I wasn't quite expecting this, but I gulped and then, trying to make it as simple as possible, I said, "Honey, God the Father is God *above* you; God the Son is God *with* you; and God the Holy Spirit is God *in* you." I was relieved when the child was gravely thoughtful for a moment, and then said happily, "Oh, I see." (The word *Trinity* is not in the Bible, but the picture of God in His tri-unity is certainly there. The word *Trinity* puts in a capsule what the Bible says throughout.)

Then I went on to explain how God comes to live in us by His Holy Spirit, when we ask Jesus to wash away our sins, come into our hearts, and give us new life. I used the very familiar passage of Revelation 3:20, and explained that Jesus is knocking at the door of the heart of every man, woman, girl, or boy, but that He can't come in unless the door is opened to Him. I explained how God had purposely made our heart's door with a handle only on the inside. The little girl listened for a moment, and then said, "I think I hear Him knocking!"

"Well, what are you going to say to Him?"

She quickly said, "Come on in, Jesus!"

Again she listened, and said a little doubtfully, "I think I still hear Him knocking!"

"Are you sure?" I asked.

After a moment's hesitation, she said, "No, He's in!"

Simple, wasn't it? Yet from experience, I know Jesus did come in, and that little child's life will not be the same because the Holy Spirit is now living in her. Never assume that a child is too young to understand things about God.

When should you tell your child about Jesus? If your child is old enough to know that she loves her mother and father, she is old enough to love Jesus. And if she is showing an interest in spiritual things, you should share just as much as she is ready to listen to. Every youngster is different, but they usually are much more interested and ready to hear about God than we expect them to be.

Simplicity in Christ

After all, the Gospel, the Good News of Jesus, is simple, isn't it? Paul was concerned about his friends at Corinth lest they should lose the "simplicity that is in Christ" (2 Corinthians 11:3). It is just as simple for adults as for children.

We used to have a radio broadcast in which we answered questions which were telephoned in. Dennis was telling our listeners how simple it is to become a Christian, and quoted the Scripture, "Believe in the Lord Jesus Christ and you will be saved." A listener called up and took him to task for making it *too* simple. He hadn't given a thorough explanation about the blood of Jesus, she said; and he hadn't explained about the atonement.

Dennis was a bit crestfallen as we left for lunch. "Maybe I did make it too simple," he said sadly. As we were waiting at a traffic light in downtown Seattle, a large panel truck drove slowly in front of us. On its side in large letters was written: BELIEVE IN THE LORD JESUS CHRIST AND YOU WILL BE SAVED! We both got the message, and began to laugh and praise God, who often picks unusual ways to speak to His kids!

It's certainly important to realize that God forgives us our sins, not just once, but many times, and that we need to confess our sins to Him. It's important to understand, as much as we can, what His death on Calvary meant in terms of defeating the enemy, and that He poured out His life blood for us, to clean away our sin and guilt. It's important to understand these things as fully as we are able, but the most important thing is that we "call upon the Name of the Lord." If we say, "Help me, Lord Jesus!" He will hear us, and rescue us, and be our Good Shepherd.

It's a great privilege to be a mother. It's a high calling. Together with your husband, you have the opportunity to lead your children to Jesus Christ, just as you have been doing. If your child's first six years are filled with the love and security a mother and father can give, in addition to Christian upbringing and experience of Christ, he or she will have the best start possible.

You can then claim the Scripture in Proverbs 22:6, "Train up a child in the way he should go"—that's your part— "and when he is old, he will not depart from it"—that's God's part. Since you've done your part, God will certainly do His. Happy mothering!

33

Who Moved?

Dear Rita,

For the last six months, the joy and power in my life seem to have vanished into thin air like a puff of smoke. I'm sure the Spirit-filled life is not supposed to be the struggle mine has become. What's gone wrong?

Dear Struggling Christian,

I heard a story some time ago of a husband and wife who were driving along in their car. She was sitting way over near her door, while he was in the driver's seat.

"You know, dear," she said, "it seems to me you are not as affectionate as you were when we were courting, or when we were first married. You used to put your arm around me sometimes, or hold my hand. Now we seem to be separated somehow."

The husband looked at his wife with a wry grin. "Well, I haven't moved," he said.

Ask yourself the same question about Jesus. He has never left the driver's seat, but are you sitting as close to him as you used to? Jesus said, ". . . I will never leave you, nor forsake you" (Hebrew 13:5, author's paraphrase).

A young person came to me with a question like yours, and the Lord inspired me to ask her, "What were you doing then that you're not doing now?" She thought a moment and got the point. You could reverse that and get additional insight. "What are you doing now that you weren't doing then?"

In his book *High Adventure,* George Otis compares the Christian life to a car driving up a very steep mountain, but having no brakes! In other words, a Christian must be moving on with God, or he will be rolling backwards.

As we move on in the Spirit, the Lord Jesus is able to show us old habit patterns and psychological hang-ups that need to be changed. This may be what you are experiencing. God wants you to go on with Him, but there may be things in your life He isn't happy with and that He wants changed. As you are obedient, that wonderful love relationship will return, more heightened than ever.

The greatest experience we can have in this life is to know the presence of God. Nothing is worth losing that—not even for a short time. When you miss His presence and fellowship, that's like a spiritual thermometer built into the center of your being, warning you that something is wrong—so that you can do something about it.

Let Jesus take the struggle out of your life. Stick close to the Driver!

34

Can a Woman Be Saved Through Childbearing?

Dear Rita,

What does the Scripture mean when it says a woman shall be saved through childbearing? It sounds as if unless a woman bears children, she can't be given eternal life. I know this must not be the proper interpretation, but since I'm childless, this verse bothers me.

Dear Bothered,

I know of a group who actually teach this, and that's a good example of why it is important not to base a doctrine on one or two lone Scriptures lifted out of the Bible. For a teaching to be valid, it must be upheld throughout the whole of the Scriptures in the Old and New Testaments. I once read this statement, "Look for the truth that makes all Scriptures compatible [not contradictory], rather than that which makes a Scripture compatible to your way of thinking."

Look again at the verse to which you are referring, "But she [woman] will be saved through the childbearing, if they remain in faith, and love, and holiness and self-control" (1 Timothy 2:15, author's paraphrase). Obviously this cannot mean that women are saved, not by the blood of Jesus, but by their own suffering in bearing children. This would contradict the rest of the Scripture, and bring us right back to being saved by our own efforts, making up for our own sins. This cannot be the meaning of the passage.

What then does it mean? Many commentators and translators take it to mean simply, "She will be brought safely through the danger and pain of childbirth." The word for *saved* in Greek doesn't just refer to spiritual salvation, it also means "bring out safely," "protect." When human beings broke fellowship with God at the very beginning, one of the results was that childbearing became painful and dangerous. The letter to Timothy may be saying that by faith in Jesus, a woman will be protected and brought safely through. But the little Greek word *dia*, "through," can be used in different ways. It can mean "through" in the sense of "during," and it can also mean "by means of."

Note that the passage speaks not just of "childbearing," but of "the childbearing." May not this refer to the great "Childbearing," that is, Mary's bearing Jesus? (Some commentators have thought so. A footnote in the New English Bible reads, in part, "Or saved through the Birth of the Child." AMPLIFIED renders this, "[Saved indeed] through the Child-bearing, that is, by the birth of the [divine] Child." This may not have been what the writer had in mind, but it is meaningful to interpret it in this way. The Holy Spirit will often give a deeper and broader meaning to a Scripture than the original writer saw.

The Bible from beginning to end teaches that Jesus Christ was the only Child born into this world who would be able to save anyone. It also says "she" shall be saved, speaking initially of one woman, then of the many other women to follow. Mary, the mother of Jesus, was saved, not only by being the channel to bring the Christ into the world, but also by accepting Him as her own Lord and Savior.

Isn't God's grace beautiful? At the beginning, a woman, Eve, tempted her husband to disobey and turn away from God. Thousands of years later, another woman, Mary, risked her life and reputation to obey God; and the One who alone could save all who came to Him was born.

Like you, I have borne no children. But I am sure of my salvation. A Scripture that may be a blessing to you is Isaiah 54:1–3:

> Sing, O barren, thou that didst not bear; break forth into singing, and cry aloud, thou that didst not travail with child: for more are the children of the desolate than the children of the married wife, saith the Lord. Enlarge the place of thy tent, and let them stretch forth the curtains of thine habitations: spare not, lengthen thy cords, and strengthen thy stakes; For thou shalt break forth on the right hand and on the left. . . .

I take the spiritual interpretation of this to mean that even if you don't have your own flesh and blood children, yet God promises you can have scores of spiritual children by bringing people to Jesus.

What a privilege it is to help populate heaven! As an apple tree bears apples, so the Christian life should bear the fruit of other Christians. No need to be childless, but be as a fruitful tree bringing many into the Kingdom.

MINISTRY

35

Should Women Speak in Church?

Dear Rita,

It has always seemed to me that Paul is contradicting himself in one particular place in the Scripture. It's in 1 Corinthians 14:34, 35 where Paul admonishes the Corinthian men not to permit their wives to speak in the church, but says they must remain absolutely silent. Yet a few chapters prior to this, Paul gave counsel about Corinthian women being under proper headship, but implied that these same women may pray and prophesy. The Scripture says prophecy is the greatest gift with which to edify the church, and here Paul says women are permitted to minister this gift. How can they do it if they are not allowed to speak in church? This really has made me curious to know if Paul forgot what he had said previously.

Dear Curious-to-Know,

I understand what you mean about these Scriptures and have talked to other women who were similarly puzzled. Take another look at them: "Let your women keep silence in the churches: for they are not permitted to speak; but are commanded to be under obedience, as the law says. And if they want to learn any thing, let them ask their husbands at home: for it is a shame for women to speak in the church" (1 Corinthians, 14:34, 35, author's paraphrase). The reference to the *law* is to Genesis 3:16: "... thy desire shall be to thy husband, and he shall rule over thee."

This thinking was based on a Jewish ordinance which stated women were not permitted to teach in the assemblies, or even to ask questions. Such was their condition till the time of the Gospel, when according to the prediction of Joel, the Spirit of God was to be poured out on the women as well as the men (Joel 2:28), that they might "prophesy." That they did prophesy is evident from Paul's statement in 1 Corinthians 11:5 that women were allowed to "pray or prophesy" in the assembly.

It is obvious from the context that what Paul is attempting to correct here is directed to those particular women asking questions and "dictating" in the assemblies. In the synagogue, it had always been permitted to any man to ask questions, to object, or attempt to refute; but this liberty was not allowed to a woman. Paul reflects this custom in chapter 14, verse 35, in which he tells the women to ask their questions at home. It seems to me that verse 35 explains verse 34. Paul felt it was indecorous for women to be arguing with the men in public assemblies on points of doctrine, and so forth. It seems to me what the apostle opposes here is the women questioning, finding fault, disputing, in the Christian church—trying to do what the Jewish men were permitted to do in their synagogues.

"For it is a shame for women to speak in the church." The Jews would not permit a woman to read in the synagogue, though a male servant, or even a boy had this permission. But here at the beginning of the Christian Church, when the women were gaining the right to speak, to pray, or prophesy, the apostle must be referring to irregular and disorderly conduct which showed the women were not being obedient or submitted to the authority over them.

Women's Liberation

In Old Testament times, as people began to know God, the attitude toward women began to change. As Judaism blossomed into Christianity, women were given greater respect and liberty than ever before. In the early days of the Church, as women were emancipated from complete subservience to men, some carried their freedom too far. In their enthusiasm, they began to ignore what they had learned under the Law. Also, the average woman had little education, and with her new freedom and newfound faith must have taken a great interest in the Scriptures. She was now motivated to learn. Bible scholars have suggested that since the men would be sitting on one side of the room and women on the other, the women would be calling back and forth to their husbands, asking them questions and perhaps disagreeing with them.

Paul was striving for decency and order. Decency here means plain, old, good manners! Women, not being accustomed to public situations, were bound to make mistakes.

I think another big problem was that women, generally, are more verbal than men, and usually more interested in details. When those women in the New Testament church got "turned on," it must have been hard to turn them off. I see that a professor in England has measured the velocity of the English spoken there, and finds that men speak an average of 76 words a minute, while women talk at a rate of 105 words per minute. This would be great for witnessing, but could work havoc if women in the church were undisciplined.

Paul's Words and Today's Women

Although the situation of Corinthian women was different from ours in many ways, Paul's instruction does have relevance today. It says to me that since women normally find it easier to speak, they should be even more careful than men to speak from the spirit and not from the soul. If they do this, they will speak less, and when they do, it will be a blessing to all. Incidentally, both of the references you mentioned have one thing in common: in them, God is reminding women to be yielded to their husbands' leadership. (*See* the discussion on headship in the section "The Married Woman.")

Since Paul specifically mentions prophecy as a gift the women were manifesting, we should be knowledgeable on the subject. Paul said that prophecy is the greatest gift with which to edify the Church. It is supernatural speech that "edifies, exhorts, or comforts," and sometimes tells of events to come. Another way to say it is, prophecy builds up, urges on, and consoles. A good way to prepare yourself for God to use you in prophecy is to try to allow the Spirit to guide you in everything you say. Prophecy means speaking the words of God by the inspiration of the Holy Spirit. It is supernatural speech in a known language; it doesn't come by premeditation or study.

It is not teaching, and it is not witnessing. It is not looking in a crystal ball or telling fortunes!

On the Day of Pentecost, when the first Christians received the power of the Holy Spirit, Peter explained to the onlookers by quoting from the prophet Joel, "And it shall come to pass in the last days, saith God, I will pour out of my Spirit upon all flesh: and your sons and your daughters shall prophesy, and your young men shall see visions, and your old men shall dream dreams: And on my servants and on my handmaidens I will pour out in those days of my Spirit; and they shall prophesy" (Acts 2:17, 18). These are positive words about women prophesying. The outpouring of the Holy Spirit at Pentecost, and ever since then, empowers women and men equally to bring prophecy from the Lord.

If you want to bless others through the gift of prophecy, you should study the Scriptures and read other books by writers who are sympathetic to the charismatic gifts, so that your ministry will be properly ordered. You should be in a solid prayer fellowship that believes in the gifts and welcomes them. And you should be amenable to your husband's and/or minister's headship.

Examples of Women Who Prophesied

Look at some of the women who prophesied in the New Testament. A good example is what we call the *Magnificat*. It is the prophecy Mary of Nazareth brought when she realized God had chosen her to be the mother of Jesus (Luke 1:46–55). Anna, the elderly woman who greeted Mary in the synagogue (Luke 2:36–38) had a special ministry. She was called a prophetess because God often gave her words for His people. She was in the Temple of Jerusalem when the infant Jesus was brought there to be presented to the Lord. She spoke about Him to others in the Temple and proclaimed who He was. Then there was Philip the evangelist who had four daughters, all of whom prophesied (Acts 21:8, 9). They must have spoken prophetically in the Church, yet been submitted to Philip and other leaders. Daughters like these must have added much to Philip's already-exciting life!

When a woman is properly prepared her prophesying will be a blessing. She may expect to be used in any of the other gifts of the Spirit, too, of course (*see* 1 Corinthians 12:7–11).

Paul also refers to women praying in meetings. When someone prays out loud in a gathering of believers, she is trying to speak for the group by the guidance of the Spirit. Here again she must be very sensitive to His leading. Praying can be an ego trip or a blessing. It can help people, or drive them away. When you pray in public, be sure you aren't offering only your personal prayers out loud. Don't go on too long, and try to impress people with your eloquence. Don't try to sound like the King James Bible; be simple and direct. Be sure to let the men and other women have their time too.

Someone suggested that if you feel called to bring a prayer or a gift in a meeting, you should first ask, "Lord, if You want someone else to bring this, may they yield to You now." Then, if after a reasonable time no one else speaks out, you do so. This is a good way to keep yourself from speaking too much.

Dennis says, "When we first began to be renewed in the Holy Spirit at Saint Luke's Episcopal Church in Seattle in 1960, one of the clearest signs the Holy Spirit was working was we sometimes had more men than women in our meetings. Then as time went by, the men began to drop away, until our weekday prayer meeting was almost entirely made up of women. I thought I knew why, so I said, 'Look, the reason the men are dropping out is that they are not taking part. In our culture, most men feel spiritually inferior to women, and they are very hesitant to stick their necks out. Let's establish a semi-Pauline rule. Let's say that men and women must take turns speaking and see what happens!

"The first time we began to function this way, it took a little patience. When we started sharing things the Lord was doing, I said, 'I want to hear from a man first.' We waited and waited, and finally one of the few men present got to his feet and told something the Lord had done that day. 'Okay,' I said, 'now we can hear from a woman,' and we did, and went on like that throughout the meeting. We also alternated as much as possible on the oral gifts. It worked! Within a very short time, men were coming back to the meetings, and the balance was restored."

This is good advice for women all the way, I think. At home, perhaps your husband needs to overcome a sense of spiritual inferiority in order to take the leadership he should in praying, Bible teachings, telling the kids about the Lord, and so forth. Perhaps you need to wait more patiently for him to speak out before taking the lead yourself.

No, I'm sure Paul was not absentminded. Doubtless he did not mean to deny women the opportunity to speak by inspiration of the Spirit in church. Bible scholars such as Charles M. Laymon, editor of *The Interpreter's One-Volume Commentary,* agree with this view.

Here's a good recipe to add to your kitchen files: "Let your speech be alway with grace, seasoned with salt, that ye may know how ye ought to answer every man" (Colossians 4:6).

36

Should Women Teach Men?

Dear Rita,

My pastor has asked me to conduct a six-weeks' Bible study in our adult class. I have been teaching for a number of years now. Recently, however, I have read articles and heard tapes by several well-known teachers stating that women are never supposed to teach men on religious topics. Who is right, my pastor or these others? I truly want to do what God wants me to. What advice can you give me?

Dear Teacher,

The Scripture most often quoted against women teaching men is found in 1 Timothy 2:11–14: "Let a woman learn in quietness in all subjection; but I do not permit a woman to teach, nor to exercise authority over man, but to be in quietness; for Adam first was formed, then Eve; and Adam was not deceived; but the woman, having been deceived has come in transgression" (author's literal English translation from Berry's *Interlinear Greek-English New Testament*—the wording has been rearranged for clarity). In other words, the woman is not to take the place or the authority of the man.

The passage of Scripture in First Timothy brings up two questions: How much authority does a woman have in the Church? Can a woman teach adults in a co-ed situation?

In God's plan for Church and home, there is no question

about the man's authority. Although God chose Deborah to be a prophetess and a judge in Israel, there is no example of a woman priest in the Old Testament or a woman bishop in the New Testament, or usually as head of a household. Woman was not intended to have final authority over man in the Church or the home. This is not because a woman isn't as capable as a man. This order was established for her protection and the preservation of a healthy church and family. (We must recognize, of course, that there are women who are capably carrying out leadership of churches. We are not trying to detract from or criticize them. Their ministries, however, are "valid but irregular," to use the traditional theological term, and not to be regarded as the norm.) The woman is not a second-class citizen, but there can be only one head to a home, church, or organization if it is to function properly. Though husbands and wives should have a partnership and need to discuss all major issues, the husband has to have the right to make a final decision if they can't come to an agreement together.

What does it mean to *teach*? Teaching means simply to impart knowledge or give instruction. Every time a woman leads a person to Jesus Christ as Savior, she is teaching.

The basic reason for Paul's caution about women's teaching men was that the woman was the first to be deceived about spiritual matters. Apparently the man did not fall into sin because of deception, as Eve did, but by willful disobedience (perhaps because he desired to be at one with his wife). Most likely, if she had not tried to answer Satan's questions by herself, but had waited to talk it over with Adam, she would have been protected.

Examples of Women's Teaching

Although First Timothy taken at face value says *no* to women teaching men, the events of the Bible as a whole seem to say something different.

Look at some examples. When the woman of Samaria
came to believe in Jesus as Messiah, she went into her town,
told the men about Jesus, and convinced them He was really
the Messiah: "The woman then left her waterpot, and went
her way into the city, and saith to the men, Come, see a man,
which told me all things that ever I did: is not this the
Christ? Then they went out of the city, and came unto
him.... And many of the Samaritans of that city believed
on him for the saying of the woman ..." (John 4:28–30, 39).

Note, she simply told the men what she had seen and
heard. She didn't try to set herself up as an authority over
them. So a Samaritan woman was the one Jesus allowed to
be first to declare Him as Messiah to the non-Jewish world!
All non-Jews can be thankful for her effective witness.

Romans 16 gives the longest list of commendable women
in the New Testament. There are at least nine: Phebe, Priscilla, Mary, Tryphena, Tryphosa, Persis, Rufus's mother
(also like a mother to Paul), Julia, and Nereus's sister.

Phebe is mentioned first in this chapter, "Now I commend
to you Phebe our sister, who is also a minister of the church
in Cenchrea, so that you may give her the reception that
should be given to one of God's people ... and may support
her in whatever things she may need; for she has been of
great help to many, including myself" (Romans 16:1, 2,
author's paraphrase). Phebe is called a *deacon*—that is the
Greek word translated "minister" in this verse—indicating
she held office in the Church (1 Timothy 3:8–13). She was
also a helper of the apostles. (A further explanation of the
word translated in KJV as "servant" and in NGT as "minister": this is the Greek word *diakonos* or *deacon,* not
deaconess, which means "one who executes the command of
another." The word *succourer,* which appears in Romans 2
KJV and as *protectress* in NGT is "a word of dignity ... and
indicates the high esteem in which she was regarded," according to W. E. Vine in his *Expository Dictionary of New
Testament Words.*)

Paul trusted Phebe to deliver his vital letter to the Roman Christians. He had not yet visited Rome, so would want a thoroughly responsible person to represent him there. And it wouldn't have been an easy journey in those days. We owe Phebe a great deal; if she had failed, we might not have the Book of Romans in our Bible.

Priscilla is the second outstanding woman in this list. Tertullian, one of the early fathers, spoke of her as "the holy Prisca, who preached the gospel." She traveled and worked closely with her husband, Aquila. They had a Christian assembly in their home. Paul lived with them for a while, and worked together with them in the trade of tent making. When he wrote to them, he sometimes put Priscilla's name first, which was not the usual custom. Obviously Paul had high respect for Priscilla and her work.

In Acts 18:24–26, we find Aquila and Priscilla instructing Apollos, whom the Book of Acts tells us was a great man of God, an eloquent speaker, powerful in the Scriptures, understanding only the baptism of John. It goes on to say, "So he [Apollos] began to speak boldly in the synagogue. When Aquila and Priscilla heard him, they took him aside and explained to him the way of God more accurately" (NKJB).

It is likely they taught Apollos about the release of the Holy Spirit and prayed with him for it. Priscilla must have done quite a bit of the teaching. Some think she initiated their ministry to Apollos. Aquila and Priscilla must have had great respect and love for one another to have worked so closely together. It is also obvious that they looked to Paul for leadership, and Paul was in loving fellowship with his two friends to the end of his earthly life.

Paul refers to many women who worked closely with him. In Philippians 4:3 Paul says, "I urge you also, true companion, to help these women [probably Euodia—this is the feminine form which appears as in Exodus KJV—and Syntyche] who labored with me in the gospel, with Clement also, and the rest of my fellow workers . . ." (NKJB). Whoever was the "yokefellow" with Paul must have been a yokefellow, too, with these women. The reference to Euodia and Syntyche and their problems is extremely revealing in regard to women's ministry in those days. Paul does not say to these two, "Stop teaching! What's the idea of you women teaching?" He simply says, "Please work together; be of the same mind in the Lord." This sounds as if Paul recognized them as having considerable authority in what they were saying and doing. It's obvious that Euodia and Syntyche were not just serving potluck dinners, as they "worked with Paul in the gospel"!

In John 20:17, Jesus met Mary Magdalene at the tomb and told her, ". . . go to my brethren, and say unto them, I ascend unto my Father, and your Father; and to my God, and your God." Here and in Matthew 28:1–10 Jesus is again, as with the woman at the well, encouraging a woman to go and share the Good News. This is doubly interesting because, in those days, a woman's witness was not acceptable in court. Jesus knew the prejudices of His day, but He still chose to have a woman as the first witness to His Resurrection.

Psalms 68:11 speaks specifically of women being sent to proclaim the Gospel. This truth was hidden from me because I usually read Psalms in the KJV translation, in which the word *company* has been inserted in place of *women*. The literal Hebrew says, "The Lord gave the word, and the number of women that published the good news was a tremendous army." The 1928 (and 1945) Book of Common Prayer of the Episcopal Church used the Coverdale version of the Psalms, which came before the King James. It says, "The Lord gave the word; great was the company of women that bare the tidings." The New American Standard also translates it as *women* rather than *company*.

Throughout the Bible, it is encouraging to find Scriptures in which God specifically approves of women sharing the Gospel or Good News with all people.

Two Extreme Views

There are two extreme views about woman's role and place in the Body of Christ. On the one hand, there are those who say the Scriptures relating to women have no bearing today. On the other side of the picture, are those who take one or two verses of Scripture out of context and build a theory on them, ignoring the rest of the Bible. In the first case, the woman is left without any guidelines for her life. In the second, she is beaten down and brought into legalistic bondage.

Let's carry this second attitude to the extreme. If women could never impart any religious knowledge to men, all songs written by women would have to be removed from Christian songbooks. Christian poetry and other literature by people like Dorothy Sayers, Evelyn Underhill, Hannah Whitall Smith, Fanny Crosby, and a host of others would be off limits for men. Men would have to turn off radios and television when a woman was giving some Christian information. They would have to stop their ears in a meeting if a woman brought a word of knowledge or wisdom. No woman would be allowed to tell a man about Jesus, not even to lead her husband to the Lord. A wife could not share with her husband any inspired thoughts she received from the Lord during her prayer and Bible-reading time. He could share with her, but she could not share with him. This idea gets quite ridiculous, but that's where the extreme teaching would end.

Paul certainly didn't have this kind of unthinking legalism in mind, and it would contradict the many other Scriptures I've just cited.

So if your pastor wants you to teach the co-ed class and your husband is willing for you to do so, the Scripture certainly supports you. The minister should be kept informed about what you're teaching. (I believe the same is true of men teachers. The pastor should always have ultimate direction of what is taught in the church.)

God will guide you in your decision. After all, it's God who raises up teachers, and He will see to it that His Word is proclaimed.

37

What *Can* Women Do?

Dear Rita,

I'm tired of hearing about all the things a woman *can't* do in the Church. How about some ideas on what she *can* do? I want to serve the Lord but don't know what is considered a proper or fitting ministry for a woman.

Dear Desiring-to-Serve,

To begin with, let's define what the Church is. When Jesus challenged His first followers with the idea of building His Church, He didn't point them to a pile of bricks and bags of mortar and say, "Start building!" The Church is not a building, but a *group of gathered believers.*

The word *Church* is from the Greek *kuriakos,* which means "those of the Lord," but the usual Greek word in the New Testament is *ekklesia,* which means "called out of." Every local church is a group of people whom the Lord calls out of the world, and calls together for fellowship, upbuilding, refreshment, and nourishment, so they can carry His love back into the world.

It's true that many churches still limit the activities in which women can participate. Sometimes women are kept out of administrative jobs. You shouldn't feel too bad about this! The apostles had seven men appointed to take over the administrative work, so they could give themselves to "the

Word of God, and prayer" (Acts 6:8; 8:5). So don't feel bad if you're not allowed to serve on the board of trustees, or be a delegate to your church's conference or convention. There's nothing stopping you from giving yourself to the "Word of God, and prayer."

Things to Do in the Church

What better thing is there to do than pray? Many women head up church or home prayer chains, which are available for urgent needs around the clock. If people would pray more and talk less about problems in the church, greater things would be accomplished to build God's Kingdom.

You can visit and pray for the sick at home and in hospitals. Your minister has more people than he can care for, and if you prepare yourself for this work, you can lighten his load. You might purchase a portable tape recorder and obtain some good faith-building tapes to leave with sick people; or you can lend them good books on healing.

You can be a church-school teacher, or you can invite children to your home to tell them about Jesus. There is great fulfillment in doing this.

You could start a "Bible coffee" in your neighborhood, or teach adult Bible classes at church. There are many good studies to assist you in this.

If you have musical talents, you may sing in the choir, sing solos (if you're good enough!). You may direct the choir. You may play the organ, piano, or other instrument. In many churches today group singing is accompanied by guitars, or you can at least play a timbrel or tambourine (not as easy as it looks!).

A woman may be used to lead songs for the whole congregation or for small groups. It's surprising how often in the Old Testament God chose women to lead His people in singing praises and in worship. Remember Miriam singing on the shores of the Red Sea (Exodus 15:20)? Isaiah 12:6 says: "Cry out and shout, thou inhabitant of Zion: for great is the Holy One of Israel in the midst of thee." The Hebrew word *inhabitant* is in the feminine form, so the Amplified Bible translates this "Cry aloud and shout joyfully, you women . . . of Zion."

Prayer counselors are in demand. Such a counselor needs to know how to lead a person to Jesus, how to pray for the empowering with the Holy Spirit, and to pray for healing in soul and body. With the rise of interest in soul or inner healing, a great field is open to women in helping people pray to let Jesus heal their hurts. (*See* chapter 17.)

It's one of the most exciting things that is opening to the Church, and the need is great for people to help.

Most churches nowadays do accept women in administrative positions, both elected ones—the vestry or board of trustees—or salaried staff positions, such as secretary, receptionist, or business administrator. If this is your field, by all means get into it as the Lord leads you. Of course, there is administrative work in leading women's organizations such as Aglow Fellowship, Lydia Intercessors (founded in England), Christian women's clubs, to mention a few.

Then there are more "domestic" kinds of jobs. Don't look down on these as "women's work," as they are very important. There is the "Dorcas ministry." Dorcas used her sewing talent to clothe the poor widows and their children and other needy people in the seaport city of Joppa. She died suddenly one day. Peter came several days later and raised her from the dead (Acts 9:36–41). Obviously, God wanted her work to continue! Women through the years have been inspired to help others in this same way, after reading about a disciple named Dorcas.

In some churches, women work in what is called the Altar Guild. Their ministry is similar to that of the Levitical priests of the Old Testament who were chosen to care for the

tabernacle, which was the focal place of worship. They see
to it that the appointments of the sanctuary are clean and in
order.

Are you an amateur florist? You can serve the Lord by
making the church beautiful. This can be a double ministry,
since in many churches the flowers are taken from the altar
and carried to those who are sick.

Perhaps you are called to a ministry of hospitality, making your home available to travelers, missionaries, or visiting speakers. A Seattle couple built two or three extra bed-
rooms onto their home to be used for this purpose. The
Book of Hebrews reminds us, "Be not forgetful to entertain
strangers: for thereby some have entertained angels un-
awares" (13:2). A widow is reported for her good works,
". . . if she has lodged strangers, if she has washed the saints'
feet . . ." (1 Timothy 5:10 NKJB).

You may be led to offer hospitality for a while to a person
who needs a home and the love that goes with it. There are a
lot of young people who sorely need this kind of help. But
be careful. Be sure you are called to this work, and be sure
the people you take in are those the Lord sends, otherwise
you can have heartache and trouble.

What You Can Do Outside the Church

Now look at some of the possibilities for a woman on a
wider scope, besides serving in the local church.

Perhaps you can write, or would like to try your hand at
it. A book or a magazine article is a wonderful way to reach
a large number of people. The world needs more Christians
who will provide the general public with good literature,
and also get their faith across in an indirect way. Or you
may want to try writing your own story. There are several
excellent Christian women's magazines that might be interested. *Today's Christian Woman, Aglow,* and *Virtue* are

three that come to mind. When you're talking with someone you may not see again, and know you haven't said quite all you wanted to, it's nice to be able to give them a copy of your testimony in a magazine article or reprint.

Do you love languages? The Wycliffe Bible Translators may have a job for you. Even though portions of the New Testament have been translated into nearly a thousand languages, it is estimated there are still some four thousand languages to go to spread the Gospel throughout the world before the return of Jesus Christ. Jesus said, "And this gospel of the kingdom shall be preached in all the world for a witness unto all nations; and then shall the end come" (Matthew 24:14).

Christian artists are needed to help turn the trend from the weird to the beautiful. If you are not an artist, perhaps you are skilled in crafts. Connie, a friend of mine whose father was an artist, never felt she had the talent he had and was discouraged from even trying. After she received the power of the Holy Spirit, she began to use the little artistic ability she had ignored. Connie's house now is creatively decorated with cardboard collage plaques, decoupage pictures from old masters' prints, or even especially meaningful birthday or Christmas cards, dried flower arrangements, and so forth. For quite some time she taught a Bible class in conjunction with crafts for the "Creative Woman." Now she and her husband own and manage a Christian bookstore. Women who never believed they had any artistic ability are amazed at what they can learn to do with God's help. Edith Schaeffer's *Hidden Arts* elaborates on such talents. Dawn, another friend, makes interesting clay-baked crosses, which are original and are offered for sale in many Seattle boutiques. And Jane paints words like LOVE and JOY on driftwood or smooth stones she brings home from the beach.

If you have even a small amount of musical talent, God can put it to good use. An increasing number of people with little or no musical training have found the Holy Spirit giving them new songs and choruses, inspiring many thousands of people. As my husband and I travel, we are constantly learning many such new songs. I particularly enjoy singing Scripture set to music.

Perhaps you have a pleasing voice and personality. You might take a course in communications to determine if you are talented in the field of radio or television. The growing number of Christian TV stations will be looking for some good talent and programming. Then there are the great Christian TV broadcasts, such as "The 700 Club," the "PTL Club," and "100 Huntley Street" (in Canada). I know there is interest in Christian versions of the "soap opera" to speak to the viewing public.

How's that for some *dos* instead of *don'ts*? These are just a few ideas. There are certainly many more, including some very important ones I haven't mentioned. Too, there are numerous professions you can be trained for which can work in the Church, or in conjunction with it. I'm sure now that you'll think of others.

Epilogue

Dear Reader,

Now is my chance to write *you* a letter. I've enjoyed trying to give these answers. Maybe you have been asking questions like these, and if so, I hope I have helped you.

Perhaps you are in a situation similar to some discussed in these pages, yet my answer doesn't seem the right one for you. Don't be discouraged. Each life is different.

John 16:13, 14 proclaims the Holy Spirit will lead you into all truth. So ask the Lord about it. Let Him give you the answer. Whatever your unique problem, the Lord Jesus has the solution, and the Holy Spirit is here to reveal Jesus' words to you.

May God bless you. *Maranatha!*